A YEAR
AT KILLINGTON HALL

The 1876 Diary of Agnes Ann Kendal -

life in Victorian England through the eyes of a farmer's daughter.

edited, introduced
and with additional material
by
Judith M.S. Robinson

line drawings
by
Astri J. Robinson

published by Judith M.S. Robinson,
with assistance from the Curwen Archives Trust.

2004

copyright: Judith M.S. Robinson, 2004

Published by

Judith M.S. Robinson,
3, Abbey Drive, Natland, near Kendal, LA9 7QN,

2004

ISBN 0-9549177-0-7

Printed by Stramongate Press Ltd
Aynam Mills, Little Aynam, Kendal, Cumbria LA9 7AH
TEL. 01539 720448

Front cover : Killington Hall,1922.
Photograph courtesy of Sedbergh & District History Society.

Contents

	page
Acknowledgements	5
Introduction	7
Sketch map	6
January	15
The Kendal Family	20
February	25
A Grand Wedding	30
March	32
Spelling Bees	36
April	38
The Village School	44
May	47
A Contemporary Diary	52
The Vale of Lune Chapel	54
June	55
Orton Pot Fair	60
July	61
James Wharton & Son	67
August	69
The Kendal Exhibition	77
September	79
A family wedding	83
October	84
The Uptons and Dormers of Ingmire Hall	89
November	90
The Parsonage	96
Dr Milburn's lecture	97
December	98
Christmas	103
'Memoranda'	105
Epilogue	107
Sources	108
Index	109

Acknowledgements

I am grateful

to the late Mrs Joan S. Wharton and her daughter Helen Lawson, (granddaughter of Jim Wharton) for the loan of the diary and for permission to transcribe and publish it;
to Sedbergh & District History Society for permission to use the extracts from the diary of William Pooley Blacow;
to Mr Paul Weaver (a distant relative of the diarist) for his help in tracing the family tree of the Kendals;
and to Mr William Kendal (grandson of John Kendal) and his wife for providing additional information.

I thank, for the loan of photographs and permission to use them:

Sedbergh & District History Society,
Mr Percy Duff (The Margaret Duff Collection),
Mr John Falshaw of Orton,
Mrs A. Helen Lawson,
Mr Mike Moon of Silverdale,
Mr Colin Wren of Tebay.

I also thank my daughter Astri Robinson for the line drawings.

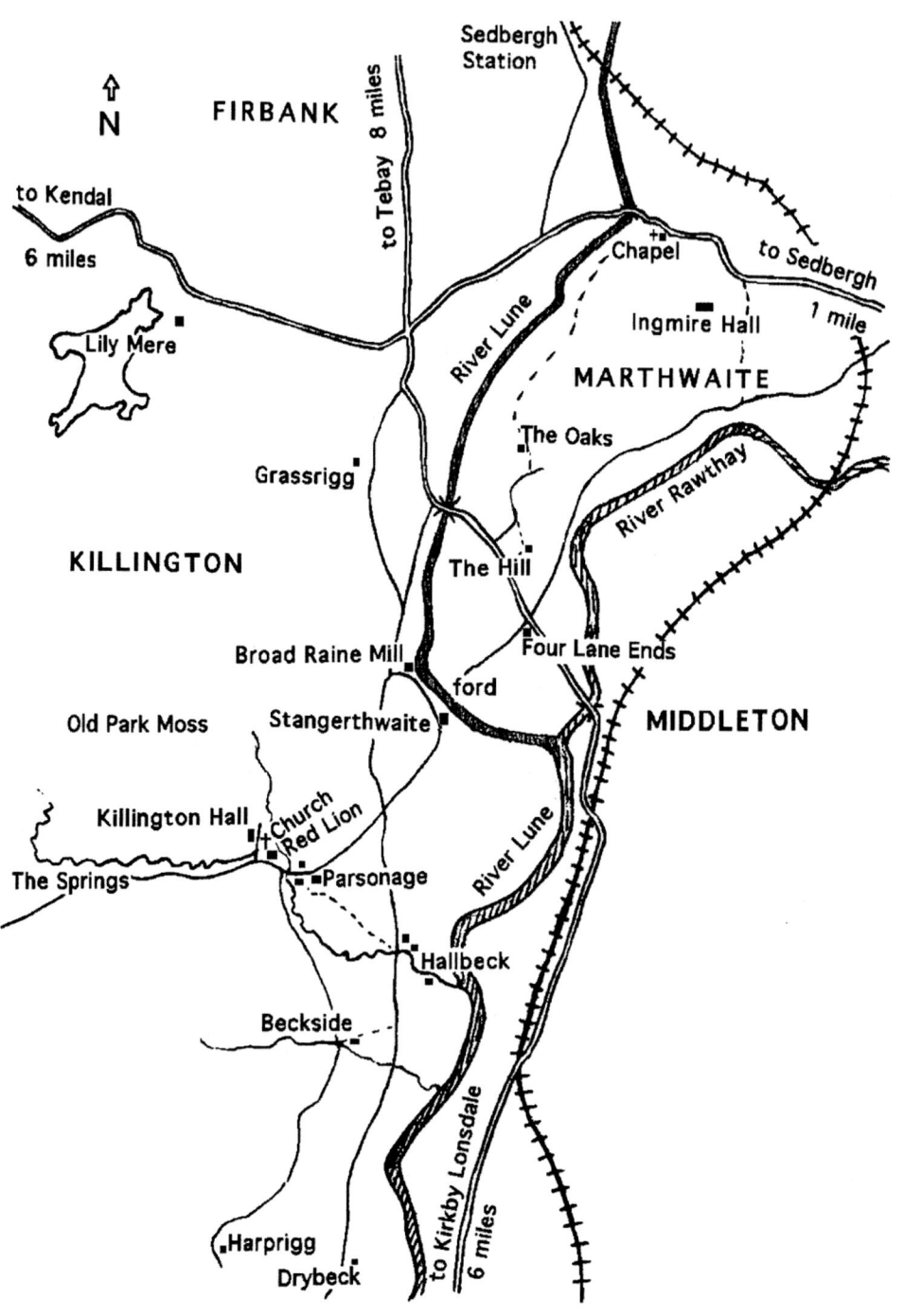

Introduction

Agnes Ann Kendal was the youngest daughter of Robert Kendal, tenant of Killington Hall Farm, Westmorland. In 1876, she was living at home with her parents and one sister and brother. Agnes Ann's diary for 1876 is the only one extant. It is written in a small printed book (Blackwood's Diary) which, according to tradition in the Wharton family, was a gift to Agnes Ann from Jim Wharton of Tebay. Jim was courting her at that time and later married her. The dairy passed to Jim's son (by his second marriage after Agnes Ann's untimely death) and then to his daughter-in-law, the late Mrs. Joan S. Wharton. Mrs Wharton, who was my Aunt, kindly lent me the diary and allowed me to transcribe it. Intrigued by the many people and events mentioned, I have researched the events in the comtemporary local newspaper and tried to identify the people by comparing clues in the text with census and other records.

Agnes Ann kept the diary almost daily throughout the year, usually writing enough to fill the space allotted for each day. She filled the spare pages at the beginning and end with brief notes on the sermons she heard and a few other items, such as a recipe and an address.

This book contains an edited transcript of the diary divided into months, interspersed with extracts from other sources or pieces written by me, as background. The results of my research are set out in a family tree and in footnotes. Where possible, I have stated the approximate ages in 1876 of people mentioned, in order to give a clearer impression of the social interactions. The transcript follows the original spelling but I have added punctuation and capital letters. Words added by me for clarity or where Agnes Ann abbreviated a name to initials, are shown in italics and in square brackets. The daily entries often included comments of a religious nature, when Agnes Ann resolved to read the bible more or regretted her carelessness or bad temper. Most of these comments have been omitted from the transcript, because they are private and repetitive, but a few have been included so as to give a full picture of Agnes Ann's life and character. In the sections between the months, Agnes Ann's own words are shown in script and my words in standard text.

I refer to the diarist as 'Agnes Ann' rather than just 'Agnes' because I believe that was how she was known to her contemporaries. In this branch of the family, the surname was usually spelt 'Kendal'. This spelling was used in offical records for Agnes Ann Kendal but Agnes Ann herself spelt it 'Kendall', and signed her name "Agness Ann Kendall".

Introduction

Killington

The parish of Killington was formerly a part or chapelry of the old parish of Kirkby Lonsdale in Westmorland (now Cumbria). It adjoins the chapelries of Old Hutton, Middleton and Firbank, all in Westmorland, but on the east it is bounded by the River Lune, which was also the County boundary. Across the Lune lies Marthwaite, in Sedbergh parish, which was in Yorkshire until local government reorganisation.

Killington in 1876 was a scattered farming community of about 270 people, occupying 48 houses. There was no central village but several very small hamlets, the largest consisting at that time of the Church, the School, the Vicarage, the Red Lion Inn, Killington Hall Farmhouse and one or two cottages. The stream running past the Hall is called Hall Beck. It joins the River Lune about quarter of a mile from the Hall and near the confluence is another group of farms and cottages, also known as Hallbeck.

Killington Hall and its farmland was part of the Ingmire Estate, then owned by the Dormer-Upton family of Ingmire Hall, a large Victorian mansion, in Marthwaite, now demolished. Killington Hall is much older - it was a manor house in the late middle ages and, though much altered, is still an imposing building with its gables and mullioned windows. A remnant of the mediaeval structure stands as a partial ruin adjoining the current house. The Upton coat of arms on the door is a nineteenth century addition.

Although in a different county, Sedbergh was the nearest market town and had the nearest railway station and so there was much commerce across the river [four and a half miles by the ford at Stangerthwaite or five and a half by the bridge further up the river]. The other centres to which Killington people frequently went were the town of Kendal, eleven miles from Killington Hall, and the smaller town of Kirkby Lonsdale, nine miles away.

Transport

A great deal of coming and going was recorded in Agnes Ann's diary, but often she told us only that someone "went" or "had been" somewhere, without specifying whether they went on foot, on horseback or in a horse-drawn vehicle. The Kendals certainly owned such a vehicle, which Agnes Ann referred to as "the conveyance." Probably it was a trap. She also mentioned a conveyance belonging to Jim Wharton. As Jim worked in his father's business of a coal merchant, the vehicle he was driving when he passed by

Introduction

Killington may have been a coal wagon. However, he sometimes used another vehicle, for example when taking his friends to and from the Whitsun tea party and when he brought three visitors to Killington Hall "in the phaton". More often, Jim travelled from his home in Tebay to Killington by train, or as Agnes Ann put it 'with the train', walking the five miles from Sedbergh station. Sometimes he walked all the way home (thirteen miles) - Agnes Ann would bid him good night and record in her diary 'Jim has started to walk back'. Occasionally, when very late, Jim went on the goods train, perhaps through the guard being an acquaintance from the railway village of Tebay.

Members of the family made frequent trips to the town of Kendal, sometimes within a day and sometimes staying overnight with relatives. Rail travel was not a very convenient way to go to Kendal - it involved walking or driving four or five miles east to Sedbergh station, catching a train north to Tebay and changing there onto the line going south to Kendal. Usually, people went by road, using a pony and trap, and the young men walked the eleven miles if they were driving sheep or cattle. Agnes, Sarah and Jim used the train when they went on holiday to Silverdale and, while staying there, for their visit to Furness Abbey. When visitors arrived at Sedbergh station, Agnes Ann's father or brother took the pony and trap to meet them.

On at least two occasions Mr Robert Kendal travelled a distance on horseback - once twenty-five miles to the famous horse fair at Brough Hill, from which he returned next day by train. At the beginning of 1876, the Kendals had at least two horses, Rosie and Blossom. In the course of the year, they bought three more, one of which was sold at Brough Hill.

Farming

Mr Robert Kendal was a tenant farmer, running Killington Hall Farm with the help of his youngest son, John. The farm covered a little over 100 acres and seems to have been entirely stock rearing, with no cereal growing. When she visited her eldest sister at Skelsmergh and found the family dressing corn, Agnes Ann called it quite new work. There is no mention of a pig or dogs at Killington Hall but the Kendals had cattle, sheep, poultry and bees as well as cats and horses. They also let out winter grazing for sheep and provided temporary grazing for a horse belonging to relatives.

Agnes Ann recorded the comings and goings of her father and brother to buy and sell animals but not their daily activities on the farm, except at

Introduction

haytime. They often went into Sedbergh on market day (Wednesday) to sell butter. They also attended fairs, for buying and selling animals at several towns and villages but, more often, they took their animals to Kendal to sell to Agnes Ann's brothers and brothers-in-law, who were butchers and farmers in or near the town.

The local farmers helped each other at busy times and young John Kendal seems to have been much in demand. As well as cutting and transporting peat for neighbours, and mowing their bracken for animal bedding, he assisted at the killing of a pig on several neighbouring farms and helped with sheep shearing and salving. The Kendals were up-to-date in their practise of dipping sheep but many of their neighbours still followed the older custom of salving with tar and butter. Agnes Ann often helped her father and brother with the milking. Butter churning was a regular job for the women but there is no mention of cheese.

The major farming event of the year was the haymaking in July, for which the Kendals had many helpers. Agnes Ann recorded daily the number of sledges and carts of hay and the names of the hay fields. The totals over the fortnight amounted to 146 cart loads and 96 sledge-loads.

Church and Chapel

The Anglican church at Killington is only yards from Killington Hall. It was built as a private chapel when the Hall was the manor house and residence of the Pickering Family but became a public church serving the chapelry of Killington in the late sixteenth century. Being Nonconformists, the Kendal family did not normally attend services at the Church, although on some wet Sundays, Agnes Ann attended 'this Church' instead of walking the four miles to chapel. Sometimes she attended services at both on the same day.

The chapel to which Agnes Ann often walked was beside the main road from Kendal to Sedbergh. It was then a Baptist chapel known as the Vale of Lune Chapel but is now Anglican and is called 'St. Gregory's, Vale of Lune'. When Agnes Ann wrote, 'I have been to School and chapel', she was referring to the Sunday School at which she was a helper and not to the village School, where she had no doubt learned to read and write.

When there was no Sunday evening service at the chapel, religious meetings were sometimes held in local farmhouses, including Killington Hall. As well as attending the Vale of Lune Chapel and, occasionally, the Parish Church of

Introduction

Killington, Agnes Ann went to meetings at the Independent Chapel in Sedbergh and various Wesleyan chapels. When staying with her sister at Skelsmergh, she attended the local Anglican Church, 'but I cannot gather the sweetnes from the Church as I can from Medthody'.

Social life

Nowadays, Killington Hall would be considered remote or at least off the beaten track. But in 1876, hardly a day went by, certainly not a week, without visitors calling at the Hall, either especially or while passing.

The most regular visitors were members of the Sharp family, who lived just down the hill from Killington Hall. Mr James Sharp was described in the census as a shepherd but he seems to have been farming on his own account, as John Kendal helped with his shearing, mowing and pig-killing. Mrs. Sharp was related by marriage to Mrs Kendal. She and her daughters enjoyed many evenings of singing and card games with the Kendals at one house or the other and they were joined by the Sharp boys during their half-yearly breaks from employment on other farms.

Other visitors were relatives - Agnes Ann's elder brother's and sisters, with their families, and various Uncles, Aunts and cousins - and other people from the farms around Killington and Sedbergh. Their calls were returned by members of the Kendal family, especially when they had a visitor staying with them. Mary Hunter, who spent a few weeks at Killington Hall, had been a neighbour - her family had lived where the Sharps now were - and she must have been at School with Agnes Ann. While she was staying with the Kendals, they called on many of her former neighbours. Sometimes, farmers or dealers called to see Mr Robert Kendal on business and there were occasional visits from salesmen, as well as the regular visits of the young postman from Kirkby Lonsdale, who was a friend of family. The Hall itself attracted visits from the gentry, wishing to view the old manor house and its ruined wing.

Agnes Ann took five short holidays away from home during the year, the highlight being the the three day trip in August to Silverdale, in north Lancashire, with her sister Sarah and sweetheart Jim. During her two stays in Kendal, one with a friend and the other with relatives, she fitted in a remarkable amount of sightseeing and visiting, including some walks, and visits to her uncle's factory and to the Kendal Exhibition. Her trips to the village of Orton, where she stayed with the Clark family, were timed to

Introduction

include the Orton Pot Fair and Christmas. Other festivals were marked by attendance at non-conformist tea parties nearer home, including the annual Whit Monday celebrations at the Vale of Lune Chapel.

The front door of Killington Hall

1st Month. JANUARY, 1876. 31 Days.

It is a serious matter to think now when I am just starting out upon another year it is a clear blank, and if it pleaseth God to prolong my life, I have this blank to fill up. I do want to live better and nearer my God that I may not have so many dark blots to look back upon but that the blank may be filled up with usefulness. I have many mercies to praise God for, and for which I have done nothing for yet but with His help I am now determined to try. I have gladly learned that all things work together for good to them that fear God. (my I never regret this)

1 SATURDAY. Bank Holiday (Scotland.)

It is a beautiful day for the beginning of another year, and I hope by Gods blessing to be enabled the same sunshine in my heart all through the year

2 Sunday

We have all been to the chapel that is Sarah John & Wharton and myself

MEMO.—An additional line has been placed on the left hand side of the pages in this Diary, to enable each page to be used as Dr. and Cr. as above.

Mr Jayers had a grand sermon

January

It is New Year, 1876. Sarah, John, and Agnes Ann Kendal have returned home to Killington Hall after spending Christmas with their friends the Clarks in the village of Orton. With them has come their friend Jim Wharton, of Tebay. Agnes Ann begins her diary :

It is a serious matter to think now when I am first starting out upon another year. It is a clear blank and, if it pleaseth God to prolong my life, I have this blank to fill up. I do want to live better and nearer my God that I may not have so many dark blots to look back upon but that the blank may be filled up with usefulness. I have many mercies to praise God for and for which I have done nothing yet but with his help I am now determined to try. I have gladly learned that all things work together for good to them that fear God (may I never regret this!)

Sat. 1st It is a beautiful day for the beginning of another year and I hope by God's blessing to be enabled the same sunshine in my heart all through the year.

Sun. 2nd We have all been to the chapel, that is Sarah[1], John[2], J. Wharton[3] and myself. Mr Fayers[4] had a grand sermon.

Mon. 3rd J. Wharton left us this morning for the first train at Sedbergh and Father[5] for Kendal. He has taken the horse and cart and is going to stay a few days.

Wed. 5th Father has come home tonight but left the horse and cart. James[6] has some work to do for it. I have had a letter from Sarah Clark[7] telling me all particulars about their Temperance Festival[8] on Saturday. I have also had one from J. Old people may talk against sweet hearting but they cannot talk the peace out of it.

---

[1] Sarah Kendal [28], unmarried sister of Agnes Ann Kendal.
[2] John Kendal [25], Agnes Ann's unmarried brother.
[3] James Wharton [20], known as Jim, eldest son of James Wharton, coal merchant of Tebay.
[4] Mr Thomas Fayers [53], Baptist minister.
[5] Robert Kendal senior [59], farmer of Killington Hall.
[6] James Kendal [34], brother of Agnes Ann, a butcher and farmer in Kendal.
[7] Sarah Clark [19], daughter of Thomas & Elizabeth Clark of Orton, a village about 10 miles north of Killington.
[8] Mr Thomas Clark [58], farmer of the Park, Orton, played a leading role in the building of the Orton Temperance Hall.

January

Thurs. 6th We have been very busy baking oat bread and tonight I have been finishing a birthday present for Sarah Clark.

Fri. 7th It has been awful cold today. I have sent off my present for S. [*Sarah*] Clark. We have had Mrs Sharp[9] up tonight sitting. Time is going so fast has iver. A week has gone since I came back from Orton and our party.[10]

Sat. 8th Snow has been falling nearly all day and it is freezing hard tonight. John left this morning for the train. He is going to spend the weekend somewhere. I shall be better able to say where when he comes back.

Sun. 9 I have been to [*Sunday*] School and Chapel. Mr Fayers preached. Sarah and I have been at Stangethwait[11] this evening.

Mon. 10 Rather a dull day, no more frost. Father has been up to the Mill[12] tonight.

Tues. 11 I had a hearty run over to the Park Barn this morning for Father. Two cattle dealers wanted him. James has come home with the horse and cart this evening. He started to walk back. Mother and I have been a sitting at Sharps tonight. William[13] is off to Sedbergh to hear the Bell ringers.

Wed. 12 This morning the snow fell very fast - all is covered up now. We have had James again. He had bought a fat cow of ours and John has gone with him with it. John landed back from Carlisle on Monday (for that was where he had been) after we had gone to bed.

Thur. 13 We have had M.A.[14] & S.A. Waller this evening and T. Martindale,[15] all unexpected. We have been singing and playing game cards. John has been helping to kill pigs at Harprigg.

---

[9] Mrs Elizabeth Sharp [44], nee Bateman, wife of James Sharp. The Sharps were near neighbours and close friends of the Kendals and relatives by marriage of Mrs Kendal.
[10] The party (if the same as the next Christmas) was the Sunday School treat at Gaisgill.
[11] Stangtherwaite Farm, Killington, occupied by the Gott family.
[12] Broad Raine Mill.
[13] William Sharp, [21] son of James & Elizabeth Sharp, employed on another farm, visiting his parents at Christmas.
[14] Margaret Ann [22] and Sarah Alice [16], daughters of James Waller, of Beckside Farm.
[15] Thomas Martindale [31] an unmarried farmer's son from Old Hutton.

January

Fri. 14   We have had James Sharp[16] up this afternoon. He stayed tea. It is the first time he has been out. Sarah and I have been down at Sharps tonight. Thomas Sharp[17] has been their. We have, at least I have, done an amount of laughing. We are expecting Mr. Wilson and Jim [*Wharton*] tomorrow. I'm so glad.

Sat. 15   It has been a beautiful day. We have had Mr Wilson and Jim. Wilson was here to dinner. Jim came off the two train[18] walked from Middleton. The time has gone so quick it has almost been like a dream. It has been decided today that Mr. Schofield[19] is to have Old Hutton School.

Sun. 16   I started off early this morning for the [*Sunday*] School and went to see Aunt Betty.[20] I had some compliments for her from her sister at Orton. We have had W. Gibson[21] & S. Shepherd[22] tonight.

Mon. 17   Quite a change in the weather. It is very stormy tonight. We had Nicholas Harrison[23] this afternoon with the testomonels and applications for the School Master's place and Father has been with them to Grassrigg tonight. James Winster[24] at Sedbergh is dead. That is another soul gone to its eternal abode. I have known him all my life. I just think I see him coming with his fiddle to the Church. Time flies. This is Bessie Parker's[25] 21st birthday. I wonder were I shall be on mine. What a dark future!

Tues. 18   We have had the [*village*] School Trustees meeting in our house today. John & I should have gone up to the Chapel to a singing practise but John would not and I did get so vexed because I had promised to go. My evil temper got the master but he was so provoking. He seems to have lost all interest in the School.

---

[16] Mr James Sharp, [45] shepherd and farmer.
[17] Thomas Sharp [21], employed on another farm but visiting his parents at Christmas.
[18] i.e. the two o'clock train.
[19] Mr John Schofield [30], schoolmaster.
[20] 'Aunt Betty' was Mrs Betty Shepherd, nee Morphet [50], the widow of Agnes Ann's Uncle John Kendal, remarried and living at Four Lane Ends, Marthwaite.
[21] William [33] unmarried son of John Gibson & Margaret Gibson nee Kendal, of Broad Raine Mill.
[22] or L. Shepherd. The text is unclear.
[23] Nicholas Harrison, [44], farmer of Beck House, Killington.
[24] James Winster [72] had formerly been a neighbour, living at Hall Beck, Killington.
[25] A friend who lived in Kendal.

January

Wed. 19   Father & John have both been to Sedbergh[26]. John has been with a cow. I have had a letter from Jim. He had told me about the death of his friend Jim Hayton's wife. I do feel so sorry for him. I have never trusted any one with my great secret yet, but I feel I must write it down here. Well, I am engaged to J. Wharton. I have only known him half a year but it has been love all the time. I feel now that I could love him always and I pray that God may bless us bothe and make us true to each other whatever else may be in the future.

Thur. 20   We have been very busy sewing with the machine this afternoon. Tonight George Elis[27] and Mr Sharp have been here. We have had such a sing and since they have gone and our people gone to bed except Mother,[28] I have been writing a letter - pheraps I might call it a love one but I don't know, it might be to cold.

Fri. 21   It has been a beautiful day and is freezing again tonight. John has been to Mr Richardson's at the Lane for a bull which Father bought yesterday. We have been busy sewing again.

Sat. 22   John & Sarah have been to Kendal. We had Postman to tea.[29] It is Father's Birthday. He is Sixty. Sharp has been to supper and we have had T. [*Thomas*] Martindale tonight. This morning when I first looked out the sky was so beautifully clear it filled my heart with joy.

Sun. 23   It was very wet in the morning. I did not get to the School but went in the afternoon [*to Chapel*]. We have had T. Martindale.

Mon. 24   I have just been singing "A days march nearer home" - it did seem to bring Heaven so near and dear to my heart. Tonight my mind was troubled and I went upstairs and prayed and felt so relieved. I do hope Jim will receive the Holy spirit into his heart soon, then we can walk together in the Lord. I can never thank Him enough for the mercies I have received.

---

[26] Wednesday is market day in Sedbergh.
[27] In 1871 there was a George Ellis living with his grandfather at Gill House Syke in Killington. In 1876, he would have been 15.
[28] Elizabeth Kendal [63], nee Fawcett, born at Firbank.
[29] Thomas Thornborrow [24], rural post messenger living in Kirkby Lonsdale, was clearly a family friend

January

Tues. 25   It has been such a lovely day, so this evening Sarah & I thought we would have a walk to the Beck Side and when we got to James Waller's[30], Miss Blacow[31] and her intended[32] was in. It was our first introduction to Mr Willan.

Wed. 26   Another beautiful day has passed, beautiful in weather I mean. I have had a letter from Jim. It is realy refreshing. We have had Mrs Sharp up sitting tonight.

Thur. 27   We have had two men this afternoon. They have bought a cow. One of them was riding on our Blossom.

Fri. 28   Another such a lovely day has passed and wonders never cease for Polly Morphet[33] and Dick Elis[34] were married yesterday at Kirby Lonsdale and we did not know untill today and our nearest neighbours to. It shows friendship does not lie in the nearest at hand. We have had Thomas & Wm. Sharp and George Elis up tonight. We have been singing.

Sun. 30   I have been at the [Sunday] School and Chapel. We have heard today that Miss Upton[35] is dead and was found dead on Thursday morning the 27th. I suppose her heart had been given to the Lord some time since so she will be living in glory now for she has had her share of affliction.

Mon. 31   John has been killing Sharps' pig today & Mother, Sarah and I have been down tonight. W. [William] Gibson has been here for a basket John & Sarah brought him from Kendal the other Saturday.[36] We have heard that Jack Radcliff[37] was found dead in bed at Mr Potters[38] on Saturday night. He has been on spree since Christmas. How full of evil is the world!

---

[30] James Waller [65], farmer of Beck Side Killington, formerly of Hall Beck, Killington.
[31] Grace Blacow [30] of Drybeck - see 'A Contemporary Diary'.
[32] Grace's fiance - George Willan, farmer of Westby, near Kirkham, Lancashire.
[33] Mary Ann Morphet [26], daughter of Thomas Morphet, landlord of the Red Lion Inn, the nearest dwelling to Killington Hall.
[34] Richard Ellis [31]. The couple later farmed at Cragg House Farm, Frostrow, near Sedbergh.
[35] Miss Eliza Frances Upton [43] - see 'The Uptons and Dormers of Ingmire Hall'.
[36] Saturday is market day in Kendal.
[37] John Radcliffe, farm labourer at Mutton Hall, Killington, also aged 43.
[38] William Potter [49], farmer of Mutton Hall.

The Kendal Family

Agnes Ann Kendal was the youngest daughter of Robert and Elizabeth Kendal. Robert Kendal's parents, Robert and Nancy Kendal, had farmed High Oaks in Marthwaite, just across the River Lune from Killington, while Elizabeth's parents, James and Mary Fawcett, were farmers in nearby Firbank. Robert and Elizabeth were married in 1838 and lived with Robert's parents until after the birth of their first child, Mary. About 1840, Robert and Elizabeth moved to Killington Hall where seven more children were born. Seven of the eight children survived to adulthood.

Until his sons were old enough to provide the necessary help on the farm, a farmer would employ a farmhand, often the son of another local farmer. For several years as the children were growing up, the farmhand at Killington Hall was Joseph Airey. In 1858 Joseph married Mary, the eldest daughter, and the couple lived with Mary's parents at Killington Hall until after the birth of their first child. This was only a year after the birth of Mary's youngest sister, Agnes Ann. The Aireys (Mary, Joe and their daughter, Isabella Ann) then moved to Edgebank Farm near Skelsmergh, where they had a large family and were still adding to it in 1876. Agnes Ann recorded with excitement the birth of a new baby 'at the Edgebank', on her own nineteenth birthday. The boy was given the forename 'Kendal'.

Agnes Ann's eldest brother, Robert, was widowed twice and remarried each time. At the date of the diary he was farming at Hall Garth just outside Kendal with his second wife Elizabeth and three children. The next brother, James, was married with two young children. He was a butcher in Kendal town, as was their brother in-law, James Gibson, husband of Agnes Ann's sister Elizabeth.

James Gibson lived and had his butcher's shop at 163 Highgate, Kendal. In December 1876, he bought the freehold of the property, which he had previously rented. The owners from whom he bought it included a Mr John William Langley. James was the son of John and Margaret Gibson, of Broad Raine Mill, Killington and, through his mother, who was also nee Kendal, a second cousin of his wife. James and Elizabeth Gibson kept close touch with their farming roots, bringing their young daughters from the town to stay with their maternal grandparents at Killington Hall during haymaking and to visit their paternal grandparents at Broad Raine Mill.

Sarah and John were unmarried and living at home in 1876. Sarah married at New Year 1879. Her husband was Joseph S. Langley. Perhaps he was connected to Mr J.W. Langley and perhaps Sarah met him through the business dealings of her brother-in-law, when she spent five weeks in Kendal in 1876

The Kendal Family

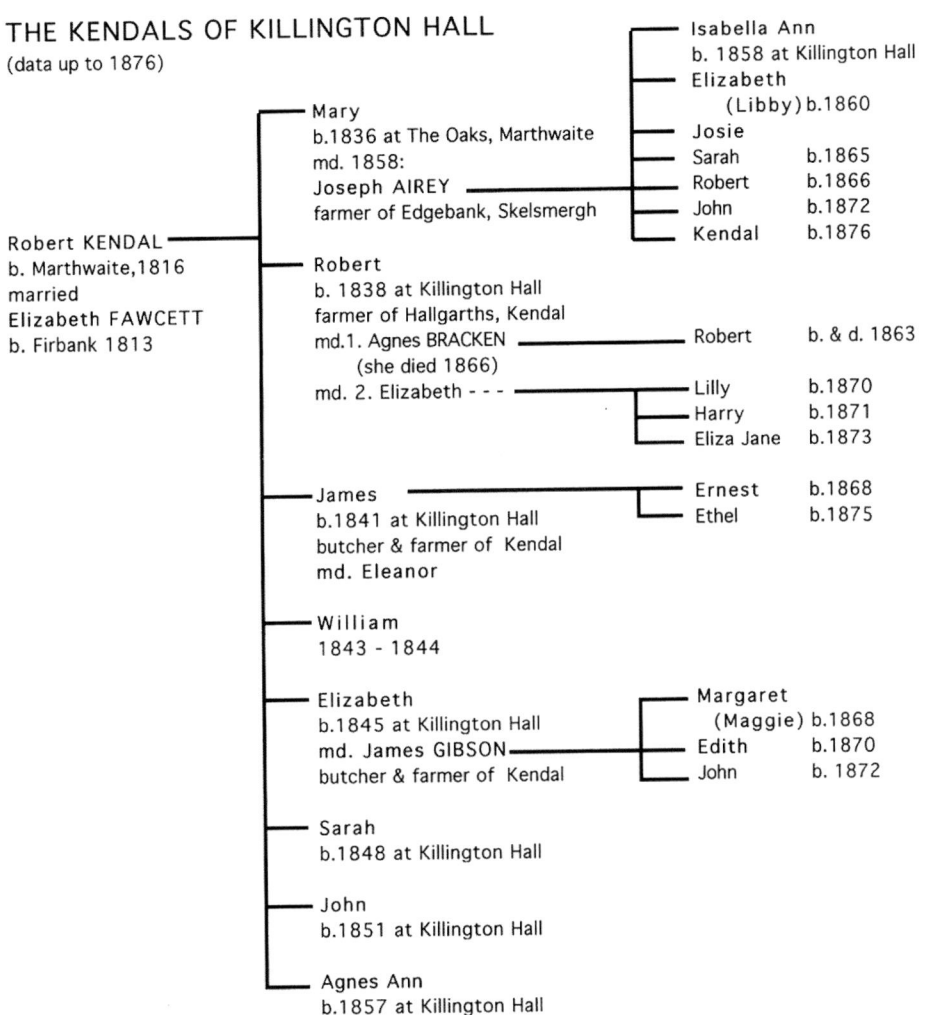

THE KENDALS OF KILLINGTON HALL
(data up to 1876)

Robert KENDAL
b. Marthwaite, 1816
married
Elizabeth FAWCETT
b. Firbank 1813

- Mary
  b.1836 at The Oaks, Marthwaite
  md. 1858:
  Joseph AIREY
  farmer of Edgebank, Skelsmergh
  - Isabella Ann
    b. 1858 at Killington Hall
  - Elizabeth
    (Libby) b.1860
  - Josie
  - Sarah   b.1865
  - Robert   b.1866
  - John   b.1872
  - Kendal   b.1876

- Robert
  b. 1838 at Killington Hall
  farmer of Hallgarths, Kendal
  md.1. Agnes BRACKEN
      (she died 1866)
  - Robert   b. & d. 1863
  md. 2. Elizabeth - - -
  - Lilly   b.1870
  - Harry   b.1871
  - Eliza Jane b.1873

- James
  b.1841 at Killington Hall
  butcher & farmer of Kendal
  md. Eleanor
  - Ernest   b.1868
  - Ethel   b.1875

- William
  1843 - 1844

- Elizabeth
  b.1845 at Killington Hall
  md. James GIBSON
  butcher & farmer of Kendal
  - Margaret
    (Maggie) b.1868
  - Edith   b.1870
  - John   b. 1872

- Sarah
  b.1848 at Killington Hall

- John
  b.1851 at Killington Hall

- Agnes Ann
  b.1857 at Killington Hall

The Kendal Family

as recorded in her sister's diary; John married a local girl, Jane Agnes Wilson and, after living briefly with her parents, moved to Liverpool to be a cowkeeper, like many other farmer's sons from the dales.

Agnes Ann mentioned several aunts, uncles and cousins in the diary. Her father, Robert, was one of 12 children. Some of his siblings had died young or emigrated but his brother William was farming half a mile away at Hallbeck and his sister Elizabeth lived in Kendal, married to Henry Rishton, who made Kitchen ranges. Robert's brother John had died leaving a young widow, Elizabeth, nee Morphet, who then married Thomas Shepherd and lived between Killington and Sedbergh. Agnes Ann referred to her as Aunt Betty. Betty Morphet had come originally from Dent and was a sister of Mr Thomas Morphet of the Red Lion at Killington. The complex interconnections of the rural community are illustrated by the fact that another member of that family, Betty's sister, Sarah Morphet, married as her second husband, Robert Bragg of Sedbergh. His brother Charles Bragg, a tailor, lost his first wife (Agnes Buck) in 1862 and then married 45 year-old Agnes Kendal, a sister of Robert Kendal. They were married in Liverpool in 1874 and their visit to Killington in August 1876 is described in the diary.

Some of the aunts and uncles and cousins mentioned were relatives of Agnes Ann's mother, Elizabeth, nee Fawcett. She had a sister Mary, who married William Bateman of Firbank (who was related to Mrs Sharpe of Killington), and brothers James, John and possibly others. There were a number of relations in America, who were in correspondence with the Kendals. Uncle Thomas, whose death they heard of in November was Mr Robert Kendal's brother. Uncle Thoburn may have been Mrs Kendal's brother-in-law. Cousin Robert Kendal(l) Fawcett is unidentified.

Robert Kendal senior also had several cousins living in the area. His father, another Robert, had four brothers, one of whom, George, also had a large family. George's daughters included Mary, who married Richard Atkinson of Castley in Howgill, and Ann, who married Thomas Atkinson of the Hill in Marthwaite. (These two Atkinsons, although both from the Sedbergh district, were not closely related to each other). Agnes Ann had therefore two sets of Atkinson second cousins, several of whom are mentioned in the diary. The Kendal family seems to have been particularly close to the family of Thomas and Ann Atkinson, who had been neighbours when farming at The Hill. By 1876, Thomas Atkinson was a widower and the family had recently moved to Kendal, where they lived in Finkle Street near to Agnes Ann's brother James.

The Kendal Family

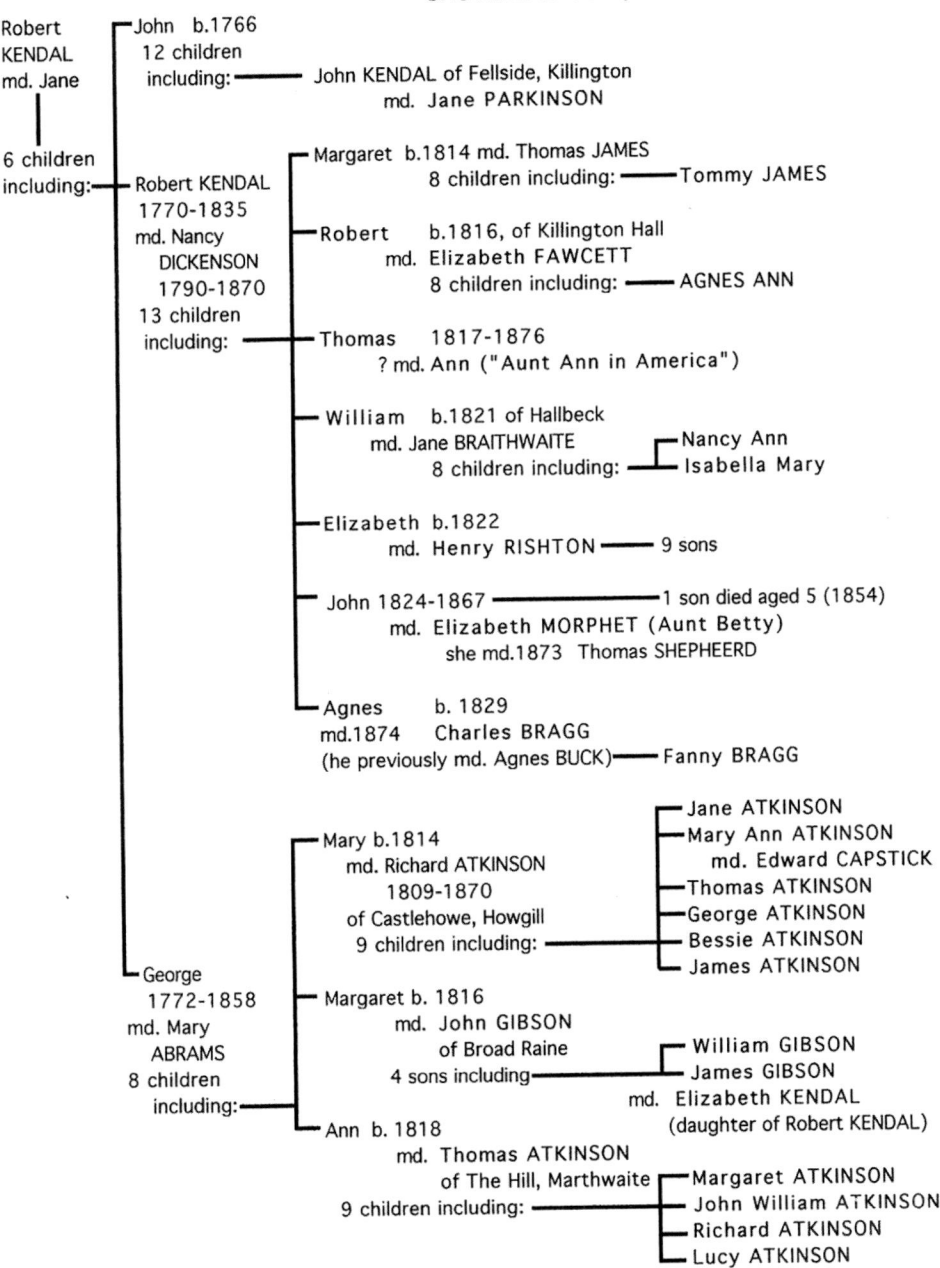

The road to Killington, along which Agnes Ann walked from Chapel or from Sedbergh. Photograph courtesy of Sedbergh & District History Society.

February

Tues. 1   I have been busy today washing the dairy out. John has been up at the Chapel. I should have gone but it has come on so wet. The teachers have been having a settling up but really the [Sunday] School has got into a ruined state. It is not the scholars that are in the fault. It is the teachers. Oh, it is their lack of faith!

Wed. 2   They have been burying Jack Radcliff at this Church today.[39] I have had a letter from Jim, and I have sent back by post our Jubilee Book which he wanted. They are going to have a special meeting on Friday. It is nice having a sweetheart. Sarah and I have been at Sharps tonight. I have been helping Mrs Sharp to make black puddings. I do like making them. It is fun.

Thur. 3   We have had, or should have had, a meeting of the trustees of the [village] School but only two came, so they could not decide for a master, and Schofield has to get one himself to do his time out for he is going to Hutton this weekend. Mr Morphet[40] is on the spree. It is an awful curse, this drink. I will pray this night that God will keep me and all belonging to me from it.

Fri. 4   A splendid day, rather frosty. Their is a Good Templers public meeting at Tebay. I wish I had been their. Somehow I seem atracted their. Most likely it is the inhabitants. John is gone to the Mill tonight.

Sat. 5   Very cold weather but fair. I have had a letter from Bessie Parker and an invitation to go next weekend to spend a few days. This is the end of of anouther week. Oh and I have done nothing of notice!

Sun. 6   I have been to [Sunday] School and Chapel. Mr Fayers gave the sermon more specialy to the children. Thomas Atkinson[41] came back with Sarah & I. We have no Chapling at nights now.

Mon. 7   I have written to Bessie to except her kind invitation if all be well, and I have also written to Sarah Clark a long letter. I have neglected again my own reading for my own good. I still continue to read a history lesson at night aloud. I wish I could be more attentive.

---

[39] John Ratcliffe [43] - the only burial in Killington Churchyard in 1876.
[40] Thomas Morphet [55], landlord of the Red Lion Inn.
[41] Thomas Atkinson [34] of Castlehowe, Howgill, a second cousin.

February

Tues. 8 I am rather tired. John & I have been to a practising at the Chapel. I have been very wicked today. I am always getting into trouble with myself or someone else. I have had a letter from Jim. He tells me that his brother Philip[42] was converted last week. I am so glad - it will be a star for someone's crown.

Wed. 9 I was surprised this morning when the Postman brought me a piece of music. It has nothing on or about it to indicate who it has come from, but it has come from the publishers at London, but I know who has sent it - he alone would have the interest in me. The piece is called " Beautiful snow". This is my last night in my nineteenth year - I shall be full nineteen tomorrow. How time is flying and what have I done in all these years?

Thur. 10 Here endeth my nineteenth Birthday. It has been a most lovely day and is a brilliant night. Sarah gave me a card tray and I have had through the post a book from Sarah Clark and one from Bessie. Postman was here to tea and J. Wharton has been here this evening. He has started to walk back. I have looked forward to his visit and now it is over.

Fri. 11 Another clear frosty day. We had Hannah Park[43] called this afternoon, and Thomas Sharp and William tonight. This is the ending of my second day in my new year. I have not read one word from my Bible. I have been so very careless. I am ashamed of myself but it is the worldly things that take up so much of my mind. I wish I could shake it off.

Sat. 12 Another frosty day. I hope it will keep on this next week. I am, if all be well, going to Kendal on Monday. I have had a letter from Jim and one from the Edge Bank[44] to say that they have got another baby, a boy.[45] It was born on my Birthday. It is quite a novelty.

Sun. 13 I have been to School and Chapel. It was Miss Upton's funeral sermon.[46] Oh, it was good! I think I shall never forget it. It was so touching. Such a crowded Chapel we had too!

---

[42] Philip Wharton [17]. He later farmed at Cunswick Hall, Underbarrow.
[43] Hannah Park [61] of Killington
[44] Edgebank Farm, Skelsmergh, near Kendal, the home of Agnes Ann's sister Mary Airey.
[45] the baby, Mary Airey's seventh child, was named Kendal Airey.
[46] the funeral had taken place in Sussex.

February

Mon. 14   Here I am at Kendal and now am sitting up in bed writing. I had a very cold drive this morning. Bessie, Libby[47] and I have been spending the evening at the Hill. We had a short interview[48] with Mr Williamson.

Thur. 17   I have missed writing at the proper date but now I will describe my adventures. I went yesterday morning to the Hall Garths[49] and stayed all the afternoon and in the evening we had a party.
This morning Bessie, Libby and I went to Burneside Church to see a Wedding, such a stylish one, Mr Somerville & Miss Geldert.[50] I never before saw the like of such a grand wedding and this afternoon Mr Williamson and us have been to Scout Scar[51] although it has been raining and pouring. It is a very romantic place & I have got a little stone with me. Tonight we have been to the Tonic Solo class. They were presenting Mr Williamson with a present for his service at the class. It is a very beautiful plated inkstand.[52]

Sat. 19   Here I am at home again. It is nice and quiet. I like it best. John went for me to Kendal. They wanted me very much to stay over the week end but I wanted to come home. I had been nearly a week. I have enjoyed myself pretty fair but I have been awful careless.

Sun. 20   It has been such a beautiful day. I have been to School & Chapel. I have felt the grace of God in my heart today but am ashamed of myself for all this week I have never thought of God. How careless I am!

Mon. 21   It has been raining all the day and is now quite a flood. We have been very busy washing and, after that process was finished, John helped us to clean the mangle & in fitting it up again he broke a wheel.

---

[47] possibly Agnes Ann's niece, Libby Airey.
[48] that is, Agnes Ann was formally introduced.
[49] The Hallgarths, near Kendal, where Agnes Ann's brother Robert Kendal farmed.
[50] see 'A Grand Wedding'
[51] a long ridge near to Kendal with fine views from its escarpment.
[52] 'The Tonic Sol Fa Class in connection with St. George's Kendal have presented their late conductor, Mr. E.C.C. Williamson, with a silver inkstand, on the occasion of his retiring from the conductorship, which post he has held for the last three years, and under whose management the class has been so successfully carried on.' The Westmorland Gazette, 26 February 1876

February

Tues. 22 — Another day has passed and I have not done half enough. Sarah & John & I have been down at Sharps. We have been mangling. Mrs Sharp is not so well. it has been John's birthday. I have made him a present of a set of cards for a new game. I have had a letter from Elenor Sharp.[53] She is so much improved at writing, I am ashamed.

Wed. 23 — Another event has happened today that never was before, that is Grace Blacow's Wedding[29] - such a turn out this morning at Eleven Oclock at this Church, two carrages with pairs of greys, a thing that never happened in Killington since memory can tell, four Bridesmaids, drab silk being their chief dress while the Bride wore slate colered silk dress with bonnet of the same color with orange blossom. I have put two ivy leaves in my scrap book in memory of this eventful day.

Thur. 24 — It has been a very fine day. We have been busy sewing. I have written Bessie & Janie Atkinson,[54] and added a piece to my scrap book, "the shy wedding", which mother had given many years since by her cousins, Hollands at Preston.

Fri. 25 — A poring wet day. I have had a letter from Tebay, and one enclosed from Gorge Dayton, a friend of Jim's. It is a gem of a letter, worth sending and worth keeping. I have been trying to live better today and the time passes more sweetly when I do try to live for Jesus.

Sat. 26 — Father & John have been to Sedbergh fair with two bulls and one cow, only sold the cow. T [*Thomas*] Martindale has been here tonight.

Sun. 27 — I have been at home all day, only at this Church this afternoon. Mr Hope preached. It was awful wet this morning.

Mon. 28 — It has been a nice day. This morning the birds were singing so beautifully it was realy grand. John has been to Kendal. We had Robert Waller[55] and his Misses called as they were passing this afternoon, and we had two Ladies came to look at the house -

---

[53] Eleanor Agnes Sharp [18], daughter of James & Elizabeth Sharp, away working as a servant.
[54] Jane and Elizabeth Atkinson, of Castlehowe, Howgill, second cousins.
[55] Robert [69] & Margaret Waller [67] of Greenholme, Killington.

February

Miss Gibson from about Barbon & a friend. I fetched the Church key for them to look in. Sarah & I have been mangling at Sharps tonight.

Tues. 29   John has been killing a pig at Low Bendrigg. We have had James Gibson[56] called this evening as he was returning back to Kendal. He had a new pony in the trap. I have been helping to milk tonight. Last night was my first starting this season.

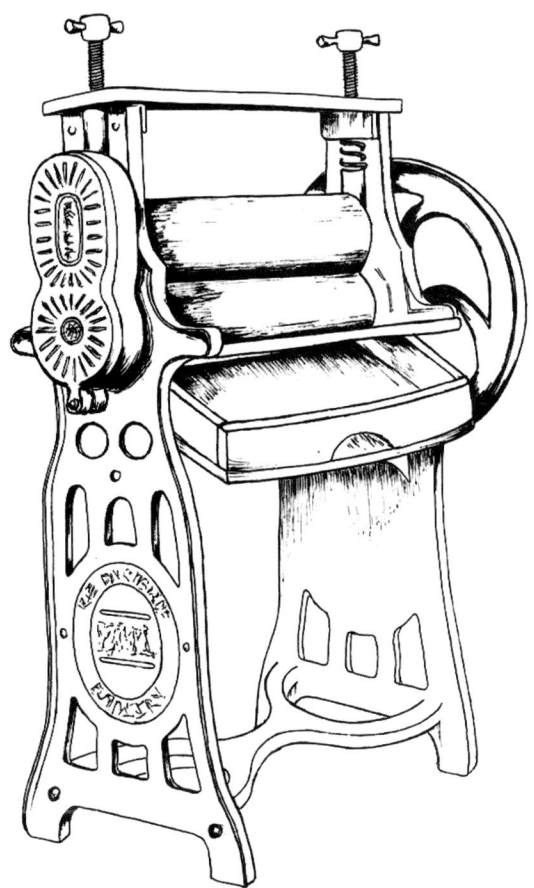

---
[56] James Gibson [28], Agnes Ann's brother-in-law, husband of her sister Elizabeth.

A Grand Wedding

17 February   *This morning Bessie, Libby and I went to Burneside Church to see a Wedding, such a stylish one, Mr Somerville & Miss Gelderd. I never before saw the like of such a grand wedding.*

Mr Frederick Somervell, of the family who founded K Shoes at Netherfield, Kendal, married a young lady previously known as Miss Mary Agnes Airey. A week before her wedding she changed her name to Gelderd in order to inherit the estates of her great uncle, Mr George Atkinson Gelderd of Aikrigg End, Burneside. Shortly after the wedding, Mr and Mrs Somervell obtained a royal grant enabling them to change their name back to Gelderd. "Thus" the Westmorland Gazette reported, 'the bride will have gone through three changes of name within a short time, a circumstance which must be a rare occurrence.'

'The Marriage of Mr Frederick Somervell . . . to Miss Gelderd . . . took place at Burneside on Thursday morning, amid many signs of interest, the church and its surroundings being filled by a large crowd of the villagers and by many visitors from Kendal and the neighbourhood . . . The bridal party arrived in nine carriages at about eleven o'clock, and the pathway through the churchyard was covered with crimson cloth . . . The bride, wore a rich cream white satin dress trimmed with tulle and wreaths of stephanotis, orange blossoms and myrtle; tulle veil & wreaths to match the trimmings on the dress, jewels, a large locket set with five splendid diamonds & circle of rubies, and a handsome gold bracelet, the gift of the bridegroom. The bridesmaids wore a cream coloured Japanese silk with Brussels net of the same colour trimmed with rich blue velvet, dark blue Gainsborough felt hats trimmed with blue velvet, cream colour feather and silk . . .'
                    The Westmorland Gazette, 19th February 1876

'NOTICE. Whitehall, February 29th. 1876. The Queen has been pleased to grant unto Frederick Somervell of Hazelthwaite in the Parish of Windermere in the County of Westmorland, Gentleman, and to Mary Agnes his wife, daughter of John Airey, late of Stodday Lodge in the Parish of Ashton with Stodday in the County Palatine of Lancaster, Gentleman, deceased, by Betsy Airey his wife, formerly Betsy Gelderd, Her Royal Licence and Authority that they may, in compliance with an Injunction contained in the last Will and Testament of George Atkinson Gelderd, late of Aikerigg End near Kendal in the County of Westmorland, Esquire, deceased, take and henceforth use the Surname of GELDERD in lieu of that of Somervell and that such Surname of GELDERD only be borne by the Issue of the marriage.'
                    The Westmorland Gazette, 11 March 1876

Killington Hall.
Photograph courtesy of Sedbergh & District History Society

March

Wed. 1   Sarah has been with Father to Sedbergh and John has been with a bull to Robert's[57] at the Hall Garths. Mother and I have been sitting up of him. I have sent of a letter for Elenor Sharp.

Thur. 2   We had Mr Fayers came in this afternoon, so Sarah and he has been for a walk to Henry Slaters[58] to see the new house. Mr Fayers is geting very feeble. J. Wharton came in the evening. He has gone back by the goods train. It has been a very short stay - it seems only like a dream now.

Fri. 3   It has been a awful wet day. Sarah and I have been down at Sharps tonight

Sat. 4   Very cold stormy day. We rather expected Mr Wilson but pheraps it as been to cold for him. We had Mrs John Kendall[59] from the Fell Side all the afternoon. We have heard today that Elizabeth Gibson[60] at Liverpool has got married. Mrs Sharp as gone to Barrow.

Sun. 5   I have been to School & Chapel, staid tea at the mill along with G. [*George*] Atkinson[61] and then went to the Hall Beck. We have had a meeting their tonight, very good attendance, very good sermon.

Mon. 6   We have had old Thomas Atkinson[62] from Kendal, all this evening on his way to the Mill. I saw a lamb yesterday, the first this year.

Tues. 7   The weather is very cold. We have had snow showers all day. Mrs Sharp has come back today and a niece with her. Sharp has given me a cuppel of rabbits. I intend curing the skins. We have had T. [*Thomas*] Martindale tonight.

Thur. 9   A very cold day it has been. I am busy working at John's slipper. We have had Mrs Sharp and her niece up tonight. Mary Ann Bateman[63] her name is. She comes from Ulverston.

---

[57] Robert Kendal [37] eldest brother of Agnes Ann.
[58] Henry Slater [45], miller, widower of Beckside, Killington.
[59] Jane [45] wife of John Kendall, a cousin of Agnes Ann's father.
[60] possibly Elizabeth Gibson [19] a niece of John Gibson of Broad Raine, and cousin of Agnes Ann's brother-in-law James Gibson.
[61] George Atkinson [32] of Castlehowe, Howgill, second cousin.
[62] Thomas Atkinson [62], formerly of the Hill Farm, Marthwaite, now retired to Kendal.
[63] Mrs Sharpe was nee Bateman.

March

Fri. 10   We had heavy snow this morning but has cleared out tonight. I have had a letter from S. [*Sarah*] Clark inviting some of us to go today - their is a Spelling Bee at Tebay tonight, but we have none of us availed ourselves of the kind invitation. Sarah and I have been down at Sharps tonight.

Sat. 11   We have had Mrs Sharp and Mary Ann up this afternoon. We haven't had the Postman up all this week. He is afraid of us - he got a son on the 29 of Feb. and he has never told us.[64]

Sun. 12   I have been at the School & Chapel. Mr Fayers preached. It has come on rain and snow this afternoon

Mon. 13   Father, Mother, Mr. & Mrs. Sharp have been to the Edge Bank today.[65] They have had a fine visit, all enjoyed it. It was such a beautiful frosty morning but has been snow showers during the day but has come on wild & wet tonight. We have had Mary Ann up to tea this afternoon. She has been very jolly. Sarah & I have been washing.

Tues. 14 It is Mother's birthday. She is 63. I have given her a spectal case, and Sarah, a match holder. We have had Post to tea. It is awful windy tonight.

Wed. 15   Sarah and I have been down at Sharps tonight. John has been at Mr Richardsons[66] for two forms. We are going to have a meeting here on Sunday night.

Thur. 16 This morning the ground was covered thick with snow. It has not all gone yet and is a awful cold stormy night.

Fri. 17   This morning we have had such a storm! We could scarcely stand when we came in from milking for wind and snow & all was covered thick with snow & is bitter cold now. We have had Mrs Sharp and M.A. [*Mary Ann*] Bateman up tonight. We have had a lot of games.

---

[64] Presumably this was repeating some joking comment, for all was well between them by the next Tuesday, when the Postman (Thomas Thornborrow) came to tea on Mrs Kendal's birthday, as he had on Agnes Ann's and Mr Kendal's. Thomas and Mary Ellen Thornborrow's first child, John Brotherton Thornborrow, was born on 29th February 1876.
[65] to see the Kendals' new grandchild, Kendal Airey.
[66] Harprigg Farm, Killington.

March

Sat. 18 A bitter cold frosty day it has been. We have had Mr. Wilson. We have had some fun with him. He expected J.W. [*Jim Wharton*] but he did not come. M.A. Bateman has been up too. I have not got much work done.

Sun. 19 I have been to School and Chapel & we have had a meeting here at home tonight. Mr Burton has been the speaker. Oh, it has been good!

Mon. 20 A beautiful frosty day. J. Wharton has been here and T. Martindale called as he was coming back from Sedbergh Fair. Our people have both been. J.W. as started to walk back.

Tues. 21 Another fine frosty day. Father has been to a sale at the Bellview Farm. Mother has been to see Aunt Betty at the Four Lane Ends. I cannot write any more, I am so tired.

Wed. 22 John went to Kendal this morning and has not come back. We have been baking oat bread. Sarah and I have been down at Sharps to night. My mind is in such a huricane that I cannot write any more, only I have had a letter from Mary Hunter[67] today and another to say J.W. got home safe.

Thur. 23 We are having a chang in the weather but no rain yet. John has not got back yet. I had a letter this morning saying he would be here at night.

Fri. 24 John had come home yesterday night after we had gone to bed. He and James[68] had been to Ulverston. I cannot write any more for I have got a lame finger.

Sat. 25 We have been down at Sharps tonight

Sun. 26 I have been to School and Chapel. We have had T.M. [*Thomas Martindale*] & M.A. Bateman, tonight. Three of us are intending going to a tea party tomorrow, all well and fine.

Mon. 27 Sarah, Mary Ann, and I have been at a tea party at the Beckfoot. It has been a splendid out. We have enjoyed it very much. We went

---

[67] Mary Hunter [22], daughter of Simon and Ann Hunter. The Hunters formerly lived in the nearby cottage now occupied by the Sharp family but had left the district.
[68] James Kendal [34], brother of Agnes Ann.

March

up to Low Gill in the two train[69] and we have walked back. J. Wharton has come back with me. The other two got each a chap. We have had supper at Sharps.

Tues. 28 I am very tired and sleepy tonight. J. Wharton went off this morning for the nine train[69]. I have had a letter from cousin Robert Kendal Fawcett[70] in America. He has enclosed me two cards. They are his Uncle and Aunt but no relation of mine. He has also sent me the tip of a rattle snake tail and some moss seeds.

Wed. 29 We had some nice rain this morning and are having some more now. Sarah and I have been down at Sharps tonight. We always have such carries on down their. I have not got much done today at my slipper. I planted some onions out in the garden. I have got the sleepines cast from Monday. Their is only the memory left now.

Thur. 30 It was rather wet his morning but made out such a lovely evening. John has been at the Hall Garths killing a pig. I have had a letter from Elenor Sharp. She is going to leave her place in May. She has sent me a knitting pattern. I have finished my first slipper.

Fri. 31 This has been a day of all weathers. Sarah, Mary Ann and I have been to Mrs Swidenbank's[71]. We have enjoyed it very much. None of [us] have never been their before. I have had such a sweet letter today. I wonder what I was doing last year without them!

---

[69] i.e. the two o'clock train / nine o'clock train.
[70] Robert Kendall Fawcett has not been identified.
[71] Whinney Hall, Firbank, the home of Mr & Mrs John & Ann Swidenbank & family. Mr John Swidenbank, a farmer, was born in Killington.

Spelling Bees

10 March I have had a letter from S. Clark inviting some of us to go today. Their is a spelling Bee at Tebay tonight, but we have none of us availed ourselves of the kind invitation.

'**Spelling Bee at Tebay.** On Friday the 10th instant, another spelling bee was held at Tebay under the presidency of Dr. Gibson of Orton. There were two competitions, for adults and juveniles respectively, and in the former class the Revd. G.D. Richardson acted as interrogator. There were 16 competitors and the spelling on the whole was very good. The competition resulted as under: Mrs Richardson, Tebay, 1st, Mr Barnie, Kirkby Thore, 2nd, Mr T.Moffat, Tebay, 3rd, Mr Taylor, Kirkby Stephen, 4th. In the juvenile competition, 36 entered and Mr Barnie interrogated . . . At intervals songs were sung by Messrs Robinson, Park, Ward and Moore from Grayrigg, Mr Heap of Kendal, Mrs Richardson and Mr Oreton of Tebay. Mr J. Wharton presided at the harmonium. There was a crowded attendance and, there being such a large number of competitors, it necessarily prolonged the meeting until a late hour.'

The Westmorland Gazette, 18 March 1876

The J. Wharton who presided at the harmonium may have been Jim Wharton or his father. If it was Jim, Agnes Ann may well have regretted refusing Sarah Clark's invitation.

Spelling bees were based on eliminating competitors who made a mistake until only the winners were left. They had originated in America, where a social gathering for useful activity was known as a bee, (knitting bee, husking bee etc.) and were enjoying a vogue in England at that time. They seem to have been almost the equivalent of the modern pub-quiz and were sometimes accompanied by questions on other subjects. In 1876, there was a junior event at Ravenstonedale in North Westmorland which was both a spelling bee and a geography bee, with additional entertainment by glee singers.

However, spelling bees were not without their critics: the detailed newspaper report of one spelling bee in Kendal, summarised the speech of the chairman, Mr. W. D. Crewdson junior, in which he mentioned and countered the criticism that if people learned to spell long words they would use them out of place.

Spelling Bees

A letter appeared in the Westmorland Gazette for the 4th March 1876 in which a correspondent calling himself 'Fairplay' criticised the unfairness of the competitions:

> 'Sir – I consider the present system of conducting spelling bees entirely at fault. Frequently the prizes are gained more by chance than merit. It is very probable that each of the competitors may fail at the first word, when able to spell a fair proportion of the words given. A certain quantity of spellings – say a dozen – should be dictated for the competitors to write on paper. When finished all should leave the platform, while their papers are examined. If two or more candidates were equally successful, they should return to the platform for a similar examination. . . By this means all would have the same chance; and those who had failed would not be so conspicuous as they are by the present plan, and so it would be an inducement for more ladies to compete.'
>
> (but not for the audience to attend!)

The Kendal spelling bee described in such detail was in two sections, more difficult words being given to those who survived the first half. The Westmorland Gazette report listed some of the supposedly **easy** words which were misspelt. They included:

cupola,

vitreous,

supersede,

phylactery,

acacia,

pursuer,

conscience,

martial,

coerce,

lacerate,

siege,

and

abeyance.

April

Sat. 1   Mother, Sarah & John have been to Kendal. I have put the moss seeds into soil today, which I had sent from America.

Sun. 2   This as been a delightful day. I was at this Church in the morning. Mother and Sarah were at the Chapel in the afternoon. Mr Thompson[72] was preaching. He landed back yesterday to Mansergh.[73] I had a lovely visit to Sylvanely Dell[74] this afternoon. I was happy all alone. We have had Wm.. Gibson tonight.

Mon. 3   This has been a miserable day to me and more besides - last night John and I got so enraged. He was finding fault about our coming home last Monday.[75] Then he said things about Wharton which fairly touched the tender ghost. I have been miserable but he has begged pardon tonight so I think he as been more in the wrong than me and I was bad enough. I hope we both shall mind our tongs for the future. I have had a letter and postcard from Miss Sedgwick. I have acknowledged it.

Tues. 4   Such nice rain we have had all day. Father has been to a sale at Bains Bank in Middleton. I sew some flower seeds yesterday and my ferns are beginning to sprout. It has been a peaceful day without any quarelling. The storm is over I expect for good.

Wed. 5   Schoch mist all day. We have had Mary Ann [*Bateman*] & Postman up to tea. Father has been to Kirkby Lonsdale Fair and John has been to Sedbergh Market. Sarah as had a letter from Mrs Slinger[76] apologising for what she had told John on Sunday and sent me some crests for my scrap book. I have had a post card from J. Wharton wishing me to send him the anthem "Jesus alone my happy home", which I have done.

Thur. 6   A beautiful spring day. I have been setting my dalias and gladiholies and sowing seeds. I have started painting the garden gate. The sewing machine has quite bit one today. We are thinking of having it exchanged for another. We have had James from Kendal here today with a horse of T. Atkinson's for us to keep.

---

[72] Horace Vincent Thompson, vicar of Killington.
[73] Mansergh, like Killington, was a chapelry of Kirkby Lonsdale Parish.
[74] Presumably a favourite woodland to which Agnes Ann or her family had given this fancy name.
[75] It was a week since the occasion when Agnes Ann, Sarah and Mary Ann had been to a tea party at Lowgill and walked back in the company of Jim Wharton and *each of the others got a chap*. John had heard some gossip from a neighbour, Mrs Slinger.
[76] Mrs Eleanor Slinger [32] third wife of Mr Edward Slinger[68], a grocer in Marthwaite.

April

Sedbergh Market.
Photograph from the Margaret Duff Collection.

April

Fri. 7 — Another beautiful spring day. I have finished painting the garden gate. I have had a letter from Miss Sedgwick to say they cannot come on Good Friday on account of one of her sisters being away that wanted to come with them. Sarah & M.A. [*Mary Ann*] have been to Mrs. Slingers this afternoon. Mother, John, Sarah & I have all been down at Sharps to supper.

Sat. 8 — We have been very busy and I have been very tired and sleepy all day. John has been to Kendal. It is just a year today since Tommy Wilkinson[77] died.

Sun. 9 — It was such a wet morning I did not get to [*Sunday*] School but went [*to Chapel*] in the afternoon. Robert Haygarth preached. Their was a surprise at the Chapel for me in Libby[78] and Sarah Clark being their. Sarah & I were so glad to meet one another but we had so little time to talk. All was confusion.

Mon. 10 — A cold wet day. Mary Ann came up this morning to bid us goodbye. She has gone home. John had a letter from John Parkinson. He says Agnes is going to be married in a month. I have sent Cousin R.K. [*Robert Kendall*] Fawcett a newspaper and have written to cousin Robert Kendall.[79] I hope the letter will find him this time.

Tues. 11 — This morning all was covered white with snow. It is all gone now but what a change from Saturday! I had a letter from J.W. saying he pheraps was coming on his way back from K. [*Kirkby*] Lonsdale but he has not come. It would be to stormy starting.

Wed. 12 — Again this morning all was covered white with snow but is gone again. The weather is quite frosty. John Nelson[80] at the Hall Beck died this morning. It was a surprise to us for we had never heard that he was poorley. John has been at Sedbergh Market & Mother has been to Jane's[81] at the Oax.[82]

---

[77] Thomas Wilkinson, shoemaker, of Killington Cottage, died aged 40 leaving a widow and three children
[78] Libby / Elizabeth Clark [26], sister of Sarah Clark of Orton.
[79] This seems to refer to the same cousin in two different ways. Perhaps Agnes Ann was distracted while writing it.
[80] John Nelson [25] son of William and Suzanna Nelson, of Hallbeck, Killington.
[81] Jane Whitwell [67] wife of William Whitwell, blacksmith.
[82] The Oaks Farm at Marthwaite.

April

Thur. 13   Another cold frosty but fine day. We have been cleaning the dary out.

Good Friday   We have been very busy cleaning upstairs today and it as been a fine day with the exception of cold, for the numerous tea partys. Uncle William[83] from Hall Beck was here this morning bidding[84] two to John Nelson's funeral tomorrow.

Sat. 15   I have been to Kendal with John. J.W. [*Jim Wharton*] was their and his friend Mr J. [*Jim*] Hayton. I was introduced and with them a good bit. Father was at John Nelson's funeral. Mother did not go to the Church. J.W. [*John William*] and Richard Atkinson[85] have come to spend Easter over here.

Easter Sunday   I have been to School and Chapel (Mr Fayers preached). Janie Atkinson[86] has come tonight. J.W. [*John William*] and Richard Atkinson have gone to the mill. It has been a delightful day.

Mon. 17   This has been a very funny day. It was very wet this morning but fared up this afternoon but it has been dreadful cold. Janie & I went to tea in the afternoon, I came home to milk and we all went back together. It has been a very dull teaparty, not so many folks as usual. I have not enjoyed it.

Wed. 19   It was Sarah's Birthday yesterday. I gave her a scarf & Mother a silver broach. J. Wharton came in the evening and stayed all night and went for the first train this morning. He brought us another edition of Sankeys music.[87] Janie went yesterday morning. She was in a great hurry off. Today we have been cleaning the Buttery. I have been awful sleepy. I have had a letter from Annie Blenkharn.

Thur. 20   Showry today. Father has been to Kendal with a fat calf and brought our [*repaired sewing*] machine back. We have had Mr Thompson[88] and James Waller in with the new Schoolmaster.

---

[83] William Kendal [55] of Hallbeck, Killington, brother of Agnes Ann's father.
[84] it was the custom to invite or 'bid' friends and neighbours to a funeral.
[85] John William [21] & Richard Atkinson [18], of Kendal, second cousins.
[86] Jane Atkinson [38], of Castlehowe, Howgill, second cousin.
[87] a popular book of hymn tunes.
[88] the vicar of Killington and a trustee of Killington School.

April

Mr Benson is his name. He comes from about Carlisle. I have been eager practising out of the new music book.

Fri. 21   It rained in the morning but got up fine this afternoon. We have cleaned the parlor and washed the curtains. We have them ready for putting up tomorrow. We have had T. Martindale down tonight. He has stoped very late. We have been talking the teaparty over.

Sun. 23   I have been to School and Chapel. We have had M.A. [*Margaret Ann*] Waller, Sarah Alice [*Waller*] & Miss M Cockshut up this evening.

Mon. 24   Very wet later part of the day. The new Schoolmaster as come. All will be green with leaves and buds soon. Spring is growing older every day. My fearns are coming so nice. I do long to go up the gill to gather primroses and anemnys & see how all is getting on.

Tues. 25   I have had a letter from M. [*Mary*] Hunter. She is coming all well tomorrow. Mr. Hindson came with the Post to beg some flowers. He tried the harmonium. We have had J. [*James*] Sharp up cutting our peoples hair. We have had a sing.

Wed. 26   It has been a lovely day. Mary Hunter has come. Sarah went with Father to Sedbergh and to meet her. She is very like herself. We have been for a walk to Henry Slaters and the Fellside. I have had an interview with the new Schoolmaster.[89]

Thur. 27   Today our people have laid the young cows out for the first time. We have been very busy dressmaking, Mary and us.

Fri. 28   It has been a fair at Sedbergh. Our people have both been their. It has been very wet nearly all day. Sarah, Mary & I have been down at Sharps tonight. Mary & I called to see Bella Wilkinson.[90] We are going to Kendal tomorrow.

Sat. 29   We started of early this morning, got our work done at Kendal and met two gentlemen who went with us to Windermere (J.Wharton & Mr. Wilson). We have had a jolly day of it. We are very tired, have walked from Sedbergh.[91]

---

[89] By 'I have had an interview', Agnes Ann meant she was formally introduced.
[90] Isabella Wilkinson [35], widow of Thomas Wilkinson, shoemaker.
[91] They must have travelled to Kendal and Windermere by train and walked the 5 miles back to Killington from Sedbergh Station.

April

Sun. 30   We have been to the Church this morning and Chapel this afternoon. T. Martindale has been here this evening. We have had a good sing.

The post box at Killington

The Village School

15 January	It has been decided today that Mr. Schofield is to have Old Hutton School
17 January	We had Nicholas Harrison this afternoon with the testomonels and applications for the School Master's place and Father has been with them to Grassrigg tonight.
3 February	We have had or should have had a meeting of the trustees of the School but only two came, so they could not decide for a master, and Schofield has to get one himself to do his time out for he is going to Hutton this weekend.
20 February	We have had Mr Thompson and James Waller in with the new School master. Mr Benson is his name. He comes from about Carlisle.
11 May	It as been the examination at the school
14 June	Mr Benson has been up this evening. We have arranged and he is coming to live with us when he comes back from the holiday
23 June	Their as been a meeting of the committ (School) they have had a row with the School Master. He is going to leave so we s[h]ant be bothered with him.
Fri. 3 November	The children at the School have been barring the master instead of the 5st.
15 November	John, Sarah & I have been down at James Waller's tonight. We have been introduced to Mr Whittingdale, the School Master.

In 1871 the master of the village School at Killington was a bachelor named James Atkinson, lodging with the Nelson family at Hallbeck. Agnes Ann Kendal must have been educated by Mr Atkinson but by January 1876 the master was Mr John Schofield, from Lancashire. Agnes Ann's references to meetings etc. imply that her father was one the trustees, along with the vicar, Mr Horace Thompson, James Waller of Hallbeck, Nicholas Harrison of Beckhouse and a man from Grassrigg.

Mr Schofield moved to Old Hutton to fill a post which had been vacant for some time:

> 'The School has been closed for three and a half months, and the attainments have naturally suffered. During the short time Mr Schofield has had charge he seems to have laboured to introduce order, and in this he has fairly succeeded. He has not had time to improve the acquirements, but he seems to have set about his task with energy.'
> (Her Majesty's Inspector's report for Old Hutton School, 1876.)

The Village School

The Report for Killington School, following the examination which Agnes Ann mentioned on the 11th May, shows that there were 39 pupils, of whom 6 were under 7 years old. 32 children were "presented for examination", of whom 24 passed in reading, 25 in writing and 26 in arithmetic:

> 'The discipline of the Scholars and the attainments in the Elementary subjects are good and shew careful teaching. . . . Of the higher subjects very little was known of Geography or Grammar, but the sewing was good. The percentage of passes in these subjects was only just 50. The specimens of finished needlework shown were good, but more girls should learn fixing and more examples of mending and darning should be shown. The singing is too slow and too loud.'

After Mr Benson's departure, Killington School may have been closed for a time. Agnes Ann does not mention the meetings and appointment of his successor, Mr Whittingdale, but he had arrived by the beginning of November, when the Schoolchildren carried out the local customs associated with bonfire night. Agnes Ann met him at James Waller's house at Hallbeck, so he may have been lodging there or nearby with the Nelsons, as Mr Atkinson had done. The annual reports on the school over the next few years suggest that there were difficulties due to these changes and disruptions:

1877 'The proficiency of the scholars has fallen off in almost all respects. The writing and Arithmetic are now both moderate. The Acquirements in Geography and Grammar, which were poor last year, are this year almost nil. The sewing is fairly good. The singing still needs improvement . . . . A better report will be looked for next year or the grant under Article 19[d] may be withheld.'

1878 'The numbers show a considerable increase but the attainments are even less satisfactory than they were last year. The Arithmetic, except at the first Standard, is on the whole good, and the Handwriting is neat and clear, but both Reading and Spelling have declined. The former is monotonous in style and indistinct in articulation all through the Standards and the Spelling is very faulty in the Second and Third Standards. The Composition also seems to have been neglected... A little book knowledge of Geography was shown in the examination but the children were not at all familiar with the map...'

The Village School

One tenth was deducted from the grant
> 'owing to the unsatisfactory report of the attainments of the scholars especially in Spelling.'

There are two other entries in Agnes Ann's diary which are, with hindsight, relevant to Mr Schofield: On 8 April, she recorded that it was the first anniversary of the death of Tommy Wilkinson and later she called on his widow Bella Wilkinson. Thomas Wilkinson was a shoemaker, who left three young children. The family must have been known to Mr. Schofield when he lived in Killington. In July 1877, a year and a half after he moved to Old Hutton, he married Isabella Wilkinson, in Killington Church. He was then described as a 30 year-old bachelor, Schoolmaster of Old Hutton, and she as a widow, aged 33, a dressmaker.

The following June, their daughter Elizabeth Agnes was Christened at Killington, John being now 'of School House, Schoolmaster'. He had returned to his former post at Killington, and his place at Old Hutton was taken by his brother, Mr. Saville Schofield. Mr John Schofield's return produced a marked improvement in Killington School:

in 1879,
> 'The School had made considerable progress since last year...'

and the 1881 Report had so little to criticise that it was very brief:
> 'The School has improved in all respects. The Order is good and the Instruction is very creditable especially in the elementary Subjects. The Sewing is very good but the singing is by no means agreeable.'

In 1881, the Schofield family were living in one of the houses near Killington Hall and the parish records show that John and Isabella remained at Killington for the rest of their lives.

May

Mon. 1   It has been a beautiful day. We have been busy dressmaking. We have not washed. Mary and I have been up on the Park and to see the Old Parson and Mary Jane at Lilly Mere Cottage.[92] We had a fine walk. This evening we have been to Wallers at the Beck Side - not such a very pleasant visit.

Tues. 2   Another fine day. We have (Mary, Sarah & I) been to Morphets[93] to spend the evening. We had supper and enjoyed ourselves very much. It is the first time I have been at Morphets to a meal.[94] We had Richard Atkinson to dinner. He has taken away their horse.[95]

Wed. 3   Another fine day but hard frost at nights. I have been to the station with Mary, to the afternoon train. I am so sleepy and tired, and it does seem so quiet when she is gone - there is quite a want of her. She said she had enjoyed her visit very much, although very short

Thur. 4   It as been a lovely day. We have been cleaning the middle room. We feel very funny without Mary.

Fri. 5   Another beautiful day. This morning I was very sick and ill and has a very bad cold. I dont ail much now for I have improved all day excepting my cold. We should have cleaned another room, had I been well. John has gone to the practise.

Sat. 6   Fine day again. Our people have swept us the kitchen chimney and we have cleaned the kitchen. I have got another addition to my colliction - a grey wagtail's egg. I am awfully tired and out of temper.

Sun. 7   I have been to School and Chapel. It has been such a lovely afternoon and evening! J. [Jim] Wharton and Mr. Wilson have driven here this afternoon. I was a bit surprised when I returned from Chapel. We have all been to a meeting at Hall Beck.

---

[92] Mary Jane, daughter of the Revd. Robert Wilkinson [74] retired vicar of Killington, and wife of Thomas Ewen Flemming, gamekeeper for the Ingmire estate. The gamekeeper's cottage was at Lillymere, beyond the moorland known as the Park.
[93] The Red Lion, nearest dwelling to Killington Hall.
[94] perhaps it was the presence of Mary Hunter, a former neighbour of the Morphets, which brought this unusual invitation.
[95] the horse belonging to Richard's father, Thomas Atkinson, which James Kendal brought to Killington on 6th April.

May

All Saints Church, Killington, & the Red Lion Inn –
taken from near Killington Hall – almost the view from the Hall
Photograph courtesy of Sedbergh & District History Society

May

Mon. 8 — Another very fine day which is not sutable for the land. We have been very busy washing. We have washed bothe John's & our bed curtains. Our people have started getting peates. I have been arranging my ferns which are springing beautifully.

Tues. 9 — We have been cleaning the kitchen room and John & I have been up at the Chapel practising

Wed. 10 — Today we have been cleaning John's room. It has been a splendid day. S.A. [*Sarah Alice*] Waller as been up with a music book which we lent her. This I supose will have been Agnes Parkinson's wedding day, if all as gone on right since we last heard.

Thur. 11 — I set Father off this morning with two cows for Milnthorpe fair. We have been baking and tonight I have been up to the top of the Springs for a pheasant egg to add to my collection.[96] It as been the examination at the School. My seeds from America are to be seen for the first [*time*].

Fri. 12 — We have been cleaning our room and the stairs. Father has come back from Milnthorpe.

Sat. 13 — A lovely day but we want rain very much but all must be for the best. We have been cleaning the shade, and had some chests out from up stairs, and who should pop in but Wilson & Mr. Benson. They were going to Sedbergh. Wilson had had dinner with Benson.

Sun. 14 — Old Mary Lewthwaite[97] is dead. She died last night - another soul gone to eternity.

Mon. 15 — We have been very busy today washing and other work. We had Mr. T. Rigg from Kendal this afternoon. He would have me to play the harmonium for him. I have been writing two long letters tonight one for M. [*Mary*] Hunter the other for B. [*Bessie*] Parker.

Tues. 16 — Sarah & I have been to practise up at the Chapel. We had Jimie Atkinson[98] called to see us this evening. He has been helping to

---

[96] 'The Springs' refers to the upper part of the stream which runs past Killington Hall - it would be a good place for grey wagtails, while the pheasants were perhaps nesting on the edge of the moorland known as the Old Park.
[97] Miss Mary Charlotte Lewthwaite [62] had been a grocer at Hallbeck, Killington.
[98] James Atkinson [18] of Castlehowe, Howgill, a second cousin.

May

move Mr Thompson's furniture.[99] Their as been a meeting of the chapel trustees. They have had a row, the Parson worst.

Wed. 17 This has been Mary Lewthwait's funeral. Mother as been their. They took her to Middleton. Fanny Bragg[100] has come back with Father[101] is going to stay all night. We have been down at Beck Side this evening. We were surprised when she appeared.

Thur. 18 It has been a lovely day. Fanny went off before dinner I set her past the Mill. J Wharton came in the afternoon. He had been to Kirkby Lonsdale. Father has been to Kendal with a fat calf. Old Thomas Atkinson[102] came back with him. Has gone to the Mill. Mr. Benson has been here this evening. He as played a lot from Sankyes.

Fri. 19 This morning I had to fetch some linseed oil from Bower Syke. We have been cleaning the Hall and lobby. We have been kept very busy and have not finished all perfectly yet. I am rather tired yet from yesterday, so good night. We have heard that old Thomas Farra[103] in Marthwait is dead.

Sat. 20 Mother and John have been to Kendal. Janie Lewthwait has rode back with them and had tea. I have been up the gill for some oak ferns, the first I have gathered.

Sun. 21 I have been to School and chapel. J.W. [*John William*] Atkinson called this evening on his way back to Kendal. He had been in Howgill.

Mon. 22 We have had a change in the weather today. It has made all look glad. Father as been up at Sedbergh today for a medcine. We have two stirks[104] poorley. Sarah & I have been down at Sharps tonight. Elenor as come home. Mrs Sharp met her at Oxenholme Station.[105]

Tues. 23 More rain today. Sarah & I have been up at the Chapel practising.

---
[99] The Rev'd H.V. Thompson, vicar of Killington.
[100] daughter of Charles Bragg (see Tree of the Wider Family), living with her maternal grandparents, Mr and Mrs James Buck, in Garsdale.
[101] from Sedbergh where he would have been to market.
[102] Thomas Atkinson, [62] [see Tree of the Wider Family].
[103] Thomas Farrer [84], of Hebblethwaites, Marthwaite.
[104] yearling cows
[105] on the main LNR line near Kendal.

May

Wed. 24   Been very busy today. Their is cheap trips today to Keswick. J.W. [*Jim Wharton*] wanted me to go but I objected on account of their being a Gala. We have had Elenor Sharp up tonight. She is not much altred.

Thur. 25   A very cold black day. Mother and I have been white-washing the henhouse, so endeth our cleaning. We also have finished our dresses. I have had a letter from M. [*Mary*] Hunter and Father has had one from Cousin Robert in America. He says he as often writen but not received any answers back

Fri. 26   Mother as been to the late Mary Lewthwait's sale. She has not bought anything. I have written and posted a letter for Cousin R.K. [*Robert Kendall*] Fawcett in America. We have laid the milch cows out for the first time. W. [*William*] Gibson as been for a parcel.

Sat. 27   I been busy all day. Sarah & I have been down at Sharps tonight

Sun. 28   I went up to the School in the morning and went to Sedbergh in the afternoon to the Indipendent Chapel anniversary. It was awful hot walking. I saw Miss Sedgwicks. I did not like the meeting as well as I have done other years.

Mon. 29   Father has been to Kendal and bought a horse, not a great value. The poorley stirk died this afternoon. It has suffered a deal. Our people have skinned and buried it tonight.

Tues. 30   It has come on very stormy tonight. I hope we shall have some rain. I have been very busy ironing the first white skirt[106] of the season. We have had Mr Benson up tonight to see if we can take him as a lodger but we have to dicide yet.

Wed. 31   It as been a lovely day. John as been helping Sharp to peat. We have not dicided about taking the Schoolmaster.

---

[106] The tradition of wearing white at Pentecost is the origin of the name Whit Sunday.

A Contemporary Diary

25 January   *... when we got to James Waller's, Miss Blacow and her intended was in. It was our first introduction to Mr Willan.*

23 February   *Another event has happened today that never was before, that is Grace Blacow's Wedding - such a turn out this morning at Eleven O'clock at this Church, two carriages with pairs of greys, a thing that never happened in Killington since memory can tell!*

'On Wednesday the 23rd inst. at Killington, by the Revd. R.D. Hope, George, second son of Mr Roger Willan of Westby Hall Kirkham, to Grace, eldest daughter of the late Mr James Blacow of Drybeck, Killington.'

The Westmorland Gazette 26 February 1876

Grace Blacow of Drybeck Farm, Killington was 30 when she was married. Her father, James Blacow had died in 1862, leaving his widow with daughters aged 14 and 7 and a son of 14, William Pooley Blacow. Mrs Blacow kept the tenancy of Drybeck and farmed with the help of hired men and increasingly of her son. Being unable to seek the advice and experience of his own father, William kept a diary of his farming activities and noted down the advice he was given by local farmers, including Robert Kendal of Killington Hall. His diary covers the years 1871 to 1875, when he left Drybeck to take up a post as land agent, at Hornby.

William made no mention in his diary of Agnes Ann Kendal [nor she of him] but his entries show that he knew the Kendal family well. He frequently sold sheep and cows to Agnes Ann's brothers, James and Robert, and to her brother-in-law, James Gibson. People whose names are familiar from Agnes Ann's diary appear also in his diary: '*Mr. J.W. Atkinson from the Hill and Mr William Atkinson of Cautley came for a day's ferreting*' on his land; he dealt with Mr Gibson of Broad Raine Mill and had Thomas Martindale to help with his sheep-shearing; he received advice from James Gott of Stangerthwaite, Robert Waller of Greenholme, James Waller of Hallbeck, and Mr Thomas Shepherd of the Four Lane Ends.

When William moved to Hornby, his younger sister Dorothy accompanied him as housekeeper, while Grace remained at Drybeck. After her marriage in 1876, her husband George Willan took over Drybeck. A cousin of the Blacows recalled that George was given some stock as a wedding present by his family in Kirkham near Preston and that he walked them all the way to Killington. One wonders whether this was before or after the rather grand Wedding with its 'two carriages with pairs of greys'.

A Contemporary Diary

Some entries from William Pooley Blacow's diary:

1871

20 June — Delivered the wool to James Kendal and Gibson of Kendal

7 Oct. — Delivered 3 bullocks to R. Kendal at £5.12s.6d. each. Robert Kendal of Killington Hall said that he had about £10 bade for a stirk last spring and he sold it this back end for £16 as gelt.

1872

4 July — Delivered the wool [339 lb] to James Kendal of Kendal.

31 July — Took 10 lambs and 2 fat ewes to J. Gibson of Kendal

7 Sept. — Delivered cows number 22 & 37 to Mr. Robert Kendal of Sparrowmire.

27 Nov. — "When cattle are suffering from the Foot and Mouth Disease they ought to be laid in and kept warm otherwise they are apt to get feloned and thus have two evils to contend with." R. Kendal, Killington

3 Dec. — Delivered cow number 31 to Mr. R. Kendal of Kendal

1873

24 Jan — Went to Mr Atkinsons of the Hill Marthwaite to have a days rabbit shooting.

6 May — Sold eight lambs to Mr James Kendal for 36s. each

3 June — Sold to James Gibson 2 fat ewes at £3.10s.

9 July — "Young lambs have not as long fine wool in the backend as old ones, though they may get as large" R. Kendal

22 Sept — Sedbergh Agricultural Show . . . Sold 13 fat sheep to Mr. James Gibson

27 Nov. — Delivered calving cow no. 33 to Mr. Robert Kendal of Sparrowmire near Kendal. Mr John Kendal to have a day's ferreting.

11 Dec. — Fetched 107 stones of oat-meal from the mill (J. Gibson's).

22 Dec. — Delivered 16 fat sheep to Mr. James Gibson of Kendal.

1874

12 March — Took Grace to Sedbergh Station on her journey to Preston.

18 June — Delivered 2 fat calves to Mr J. Kendal at Kendal.

6 July — Delivered calving cow to Mr R. Kendal at Kendal fortnightly fair. A better sale for fat sheep and lambs. Sold ours to Mr J.Gibson at the fair for 28s each to be delivered in July and August.

Extracts from The Farming Diary of William Pooley Blacow, transcribed by Mr J. A. Goulding and published in The Sedbergh Historian.

The Vale of Lune Chapel

Whit Sunday.   *I have been to School and chappel - all expectations for tomorrow.*

Whit Monday.   *I enjoyed myself but was never playing. We had hundreds of people. The pieces and singing, I was told, was done very well.*

29 October   *This is Mr Fayers' 18 aniversary of is first landing at Sedbergh.*

The Baptist minister of the Vale of Lune Chapel was Mr Thomas Fayers, who came to the area in 1858 at the request of local landowner, Miss Frances Upton of Ingmire Hall, to serve the temporary workers on the railway. When he had attracted a congregation of local people, Miss Upton had a Chapel built for them with a Sunday School beside it. In September 1876, Mr Fayers, who lived with his family in Sedbergh, went to stay at Wick Hill with the late Miss Upton's uncle, Major Way. The fact that some of Mr Fayer's children bore the middle name of Way suggests that there was some family connection. While he was away, the services at the Vale of Lune Chapel were taken by other ministers, such as Mr Holroyd, of Sedbergh Congregational Church.

The big social event of the year was the Vale of Lune Chapel Sunday School Anniversary, held on Whit Monday. A small booklet of hymns printed for Whit 1875 survives with the diary and bears Agnes Ann's signature on the front cover. It contains the words of eight hymns, one of them, bearing the initials TF, no doubt written by Mr Fayers.

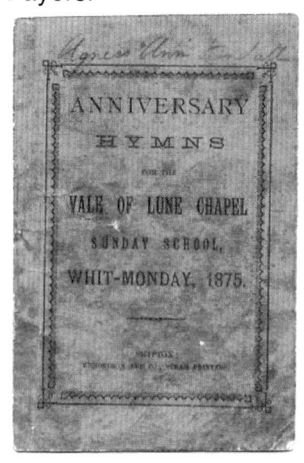

There were also Sunday School picnics. One of these, held at Killington Hall, was commemorated in the inscription on a silver plated teapot presented to Agnes Ann Kendal, who had perhaps helped to organise it. The teapot, now lost, is remembered by the grandson of John Kendal.

June

Thurs. 1   The land is very back for the time of the year. Our Robert[107] was starting the hay last year as today.

Sat. 3   Sarah and John have been to Kendal and it came on so dreadful wet they stayed very late on that account. John Parkinson as come tonight by the last train. He is quite a stranger. 'Tis a year since he as been here.

Whit Sun.   I have been to School and chappel - all expectations for tomorrow.[108]

Whit Mon.   It was a poring wet morning. I thought it would be a complete blank but it soon cleared out so bright and fine. I enjoyed myself but was never playing. Miss Clark was there. J. Wharton had his conveyance. They have gone back with him. We had hundreds of people. The pieces and singing, I was told, was done very well.

Tues. 6   It has been a splendid night for us to drive from Cautley. We were surprised this morning when John wand [*wanted*] to go to Cautley. We were very much pleased, and enjoyed our selves very much, only I had the misfortune to get my teeth hurt in a certain game and broke a cup while getting my tea

Wed. 7   I have been busy baking today which as kept me from growing lazy and tired - after two days romping one feels like a fish out of water. We have been expecting M. [*Margaret*] & Lucy Atkinson[109] and W. [*William*] Gibson this evening but they have not come. J. Parkinson went back yesterday morning.

Thur. 8   We have had William & John Sharp up this evening. We have had such a good sing! I have not done so much at playing for a long time.

Fri. 9   We have had a lot of thunder this afternoon but not so loud here we saw no lightening but it appeared to be a storm at some distance. Sarah & I have been down at Sharps tonight to say goodbye to the lads.[110]

---

[107] Robert Kendal [30], eldest brother of Agnes Ann, farmer of Hallgarths near Kendal.
[108] - for the Whit Monday Chapel Anniversary and tea party at the Vale of Lune Chapel.
[109] Margaret [29] and Lucy [16] Atkinson, of Kendal, second cousins.
[110] The farm workers had been having a few days' holiday at home, for Whitsuntide.

June

Sat. 10   It as been such a splendid day! Our people have been clipping sheep. We have had Charley Morphet[111] all the afternoon. I hope it will be fine tomorrow. I am to go to Sedbergh to the Holme to tea.

Sun. 11   I have been to Sedbergh [*for*] the Weslyan anneversary and went with Miss Sedgwicks to their Cousin at Lach [*Larch*] Bank to tea.

Tues. 13   A beautiful day. Our people have led four carts of peats, the first of the season. We have had T. [*Thomas*] Martindale to see about our going to Orton (I have had an invitation sent today for the Pot Fair[112]) but we have not made any arrangements with him.

Wed. 14   Another beautiful day. Miss Sedgwicks have been here. We have had some fun. They said they had enjoyed themselves but their visit as soon been over. Mr Benson has been up this evening too. We have arranged and he is coming to live with us when he comes back from the holiday. He as had supper with us.

Thur. 15   It has been a poring wet day untill this evening when it cleared up fine. I should have gone to Aunt Betty to clean but it was so wet. Father and John have been at Kirby [*Lonsdale*] Fair and John as gone to Hutton to a party since milking time. It will have spoiled their party but all is for the best. I have been awful busy preparing for goin to Orton tomorrow, Sarah & I.

Mon. 19   I have landed back from Orton today. We went on Friday and enjoyed ourselves very much. It was like some sacred anniversary to me - indeed it was a anniversary which I hope to heed all my life.[113] I should have come back on the Saturday but it was so wet I could not so I had to borrow a frock for Sunday and today Mr Shepherd brought me down to Tebay and Mrs Wilson made me miss the train so I had a jolly day at Tebay and Jim as come down with me this evening. He is gone back with the goods train.

---

[111] Charles Morphet [5], grandson of the landlord of the Red Lion Inn and son of Polly Morphet whose wedding had surprised the Kendals in January.
[112] See 'Orton Pot Fair'.
[113] In January, Agnes Ann wrote that she had known Jim Wharton for only six months - this explains where and how she met him.

June

Orton. Early twentieth century.
(the School on the left and Market Hall on the right).
The Pot Fair was held in the Market Hall and on the School Green.
Photograph courtesy of Mr Colin Wren

June

Tues. 20   We have been awful busy and I have felt very tired and sleepy. I have a lot of sewing work which ought to be done before haytime. I am very weiry but I hope to feel better able for work tomorrow It is just a year today since I got Jim's first letter. I can just fancy my feelings how I read it over & over and then asked Mother and was satisfied. What a day it was!

Wed. 21   Mother & I have been so busy washing. The weather as been so hot. It as thundred tonight.

Thur. 22   It as been a very warm day. I have been cleaning at Aunt Betty's today. I got a ride back so far with Mr Gibson.[114] I am rather tired and sleepy.

Fri. 23   We have been very busy today. It as been awful wet. John has gone a fishing tonight. Their is quite a flood. E.A. [*Eleanor Agnes*] Sharp[115] as been up this evening. Their as been a meeting of the committ (School). They have had a row with the Schoolmaster. He is going to leave so we s[h]ant be bothered with him.

Sat. 24   Sarah as come back[116] his evening while we were milking and what was my surprise but to find Jim in the kitchen. He had come with her to help her with her luggage. We have had a walk since.

Sun. 25   We had a nice walk this morning up the Springs. Afternoon we went to Chapel. We had the walk to ourselves bothe ways. John as gone to Castlehowe[117]. T.M. as been down tonight.

Mon. 26   Jim went off for the first train. I have been awful sleepy and tired all day.

Tues. 27   I have been awful busy. Nothing new only the practise manual and music book has come which I wrote to London for on Saturday.

Wed. 28   Mrs J. Kendall[118] has been baking oat bread. John went off this morning for the north for a few days. I have had a letter from

---

[114] to Mr James Gibson's home, Broad Raine Mill - about half way.
[115] Eleanor Agnes Sharp [18].
[116] from Orton.
[117] Castlehowe Farm, Howgill, the home of their second cousins, the Atkinsons.
[118] Jane [51] wife of John Kendall of Fellside Farm, Killington.

June

              S. [*Sarah*] Clark. They are coming tomorrow. Father and I have been washing the conveyance .

Thur. 29   Father went to the station to meet Libby & Sarah this morning. We have had T.M. down to arrange about going tomorrow.

Fri. 30   We have had a proper day of it. We have been to the pic nic at Cautley Holme. Such lots of people there, J.W. [*Jim Wharton*] among the rest. I have not space here to enter all - memory must carry it. I think we all enjoyed ourselves very fair.

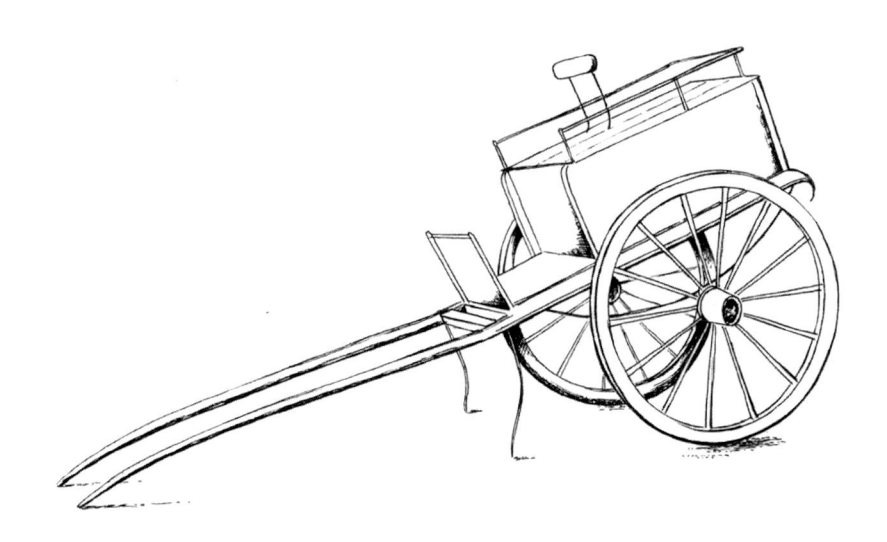

A pony trap or 'conveyance' in a farmyard,
from a Photograph in the Sedbergh & District History Society collection.

Orton Pot Fair

13 June   *We have had T. Martindale to see about our going to Orton (I have had an invitation sent today for the Pot Fair) but we have not made any arrangements with him.*

15 June   *I have been awful busy preparing for goin to Orton tomorrow, Sarah & I.*

19 June   *I have landed back from Orton today. We went on Friday and enjoyed ourselves very much. It was like some sacred anniversary to me - indeed it was a anniversary which I hope to heed all my life. I should have come back on the Saturday but it was so wet I could not.*

20 June   *It is just a year today since I got Jim's first letter. I can just fancy my feelings how I read it over & over and then asked Mother and was satisfied. What a day it was!*

The village, or small market-town, of Orton, situated on a crossroads of the Kendal to Appleby and Penrith to Kirkby Stephen roads, held three annual fairs, the Spring fair, the Pot Fair, on the second Friday after Whit Sunday, and the Tup Fair (i.e. ram fair) in October. The Pot Fair attracted crowds from all over the district. Tinkers or other travelling salesmen brought a large selection of pottery and china, and set up their stalls in the Market Hall in the centre of the village. The entertainment included bands, piano playing and a procession, as well as stalls selling a variety of produce and sports on the nearby School Green.

In 1890, The Westmorland Gazette contained a report headed, 'Orton Gala & Sports', which stated

> 'It was formerly a noted pot fair, but has of late years been changed to a day of sports and recreation...'

However, at least one tinker continued well into the twentieth century, to bring his pots for sale and to set up fairground rides on the School Green.

Agnes Ann Kendal first met Jim Wharton at the Orton Pot Fair of 1875. Her 'sacred anniversary' would however be rather movable, as the date of the Pot Fair varied with the date of Whitsun.

July

Sat. 1   John has taken Miss Clarks to Mr Scaifs at Bains Bank.[119] Mother went with them for a ride. It as been awful wet this evening. They have had a very short stay with us.

Sun. 2   I have been all day at home. Mother & S. [*Sarah*] have bothe been to Chapel. I have been reading a little book which M. [*Mary*] Hunter left me to read. I have passed a quiet and pleasant afternoon by myself.

Mon. 3   It has been Sharps' clipping on the park[120]. John has been their. Father & Mother have been to Kendal. Our bees swarmed when they were all away but Sarah & I. We got J. Medcalf[121] and Cousin Tommy James[122] to hive them. I have had a letter from Cousin Robert Kendal in America. He is very well. I am glad.

Tues. 4   We have had James Gibson here to day. He has brought Maggie & Edith for their holidays.[123] John has been to Kendal. Our people have started mowing so now for plenty of hot work for us. I have had a sweet letter from J.W. [*Jim Wharton*]. We have been so very busy I have neglected my reading rather.

Wed. 5   We have not done anything with the hay today. It as been bad hay weather. I supose this is to be Mr Thompson's wedding day today.[124] I have such a lot of letters to answer but I am awful fond of pro--asling [*procrastinating?*]. Oh, that I could be different!

Thur. 6   It as been a very fine [*day*]. I have been out at the hay for the first time this afternoon. John was up at Sedbergh this morning for another horse about Rosie's color. At my spare time, I have been very busy making my print dress which I have almost finished. I am growing very fond of dressmaking.

Fri. 7   It has been a wet day - no hay working at all. I have sent a letter off for Robert in America today and also one for F.[*Fanny*] Bragg.

---

[119] The Scaifs at Bainsbank, Middleton, probably related to a family of the same name who were neighbours of the Clarks, at Orton.

[120] i.e. sheep-shearing on the high ground known as the Park.

[121] possibly John Medcalf [53] of Moss Butts Cottage, Killington.

[122] Thomas James [28] (see Tree of the wider family)

[123] Agnes Ann's nieces, Maggie [8] & Edith [5] daughters of James and Elizabeth Gibson, who lived in Kendal and came to stay with their grandparents for haytime.

[124] see 'The Parsonage'.

July

I have had a letter from S. [*Sarah*] Clark. They got home alright on Monday night.

Sat. 8 This morning I saw such a beautiful rainbow! It did look delightful but it has been showery all day. No hay working. I have sent my Cousin R.K. Fawcett a newspaper. We are having fine fun with Maggie & Edith. How soon this week as passed!

Sun. 9 I have been to School and Chappel, Maggie with me. Mr Fayers is away & someone else should have preached. I dont know who but no one came and we had no service. We only sang. M. [*Maggie*] & I have been at the Mill to tea.[125]

Mon. 10 John went to Kendal early this morning with his lambs. R.[*Richard*] Atkinson came back with him. Willie Witwell has come to. Mr Wilson came in just as we were going to have dinner. He has gone back by the last passenger train. He as rattled it with talking.

Tues. 11 Rather a fine day but not so very fast for hay working. We have not lead any yet. We have had a lot of work today, churning first thing in the morning and I have been out this afternoon. I have sent to London for two more pictures.

Wed. 12 It as been a nice day but not fast hay working. We have lead our first hay - we have got 7 carts out of the coppie. I am very tired tonight but I hope that a sweet night rest will bring me all life to my work again in the morning. It is sweet to lie down in full peace bothe of mind and soul, which I hope to do tonight.

Thur. 13 It as been a very fine day and we have had a very hard days work I am awfuly tired. We have got ten sledges and six carts out of the coppie. We have cleared it. In all we have got 13 carts and 10 sledges.

Fri. 14 It as been the finest day we have had. The sun has been out the whole day. We have lead 13 carts from the low part of the Middle Field. I have had a letter from Mr Fayers. It rather surprised me. I have had to answer it. We had James here this morning for his horse back.

---

[125] they went to tea with Mr & Mrs Gibson, Maggie's paternal grandparents, at Broad Raine Mill.

July

Haytime at Conder Farm, Dent. Late nineteenth century.
Photograph courtesy of Sedbergh & District History Society

July

Sat. 15 It has been awful hot, almost unbearable. I have been nearly done up. We have finished the lower part of the Middle Field -10 carts today. All together 23 carts.

Sun. 16 Maggie and I have been at School and Chapel. It has been awful hot. None of our people have been their besides. We called and had our tea at the Mill & Wm.[126] came on with us after.

Mon. 17 It has been a fine day not quite so hot as Saturday. We have finished the meadow - 21 carts. We have not had much trouble with it. We have got 9 carts from bottom of wet field. Uncle James[127] & little Robert have come and Isabella Ann & Libby[128] have come this afternoon so their are 13[129] of us in the house at present.

Tues. 18 Not a very good hay day. We were rather frightened of rain. We led 19 carts out of big cock from top of wet field. It was only mown yesterday. James Gibson has come this evening for the girls. Maggie was very sorrowful to leave. Edith was in good spirits. I have a very bad cold.

Wed. 19 It has been a fine day again. We have got 3 more carts from the wet field. I am tired so I am off to bed without filling up the space.

Thur. 20 Another beautiful day. We have got 11½ carts out of the wet field and have finished it, 32½ in all. Also we have got 11½ from top of middle field but night come on and we could not finish it off.

Fri. 21 It has been another beautiful day. We have got 6 more carts from top of middle field, 17 in all, and 28 sledges from far dale in park field. We have been awful busy. Jane Whitwell has been here for her berries.[130] She never had such a few. Berries are very scarce. We ought to be more thankful for everything.

---

[126] William [33] son of James Gibson of Broad Raine and uncle of Maggie Gibson
[127] either Thomas James [68], husband of Agnes Ann's Aunt Margaret, with a grandson Robert, or possibly James Fawcett [68], widowed brother of Mrs Elizabeth Kendal.
[128] Isabella Ann Airey [18] and her sister Elizabeth 'Libby' [16]. See Family Tree.
[129] Mr. & Mrs. Robert Kendal, Sarah, John, and Agnes Ann Kendal, Maggie & Edith Gibson, Richard Atkinson & Willie Whitwell, Isabella Ann & Libby Airey, Uncle James & little Robert.
[130] probably bilberries.

July

Sat. 22	It has been a fine day but rather dull. We have led 36 sleges & 2 carts. I am awful slepy. We have got the two pictures I sent for, for Sarah and also some for Bell.
Sun. 23	Bell, Libby, Robert & I were at the Church in the morning. I have been at home since. We have had a meeting here in the Hall. Mr Burton was the preacher. I do like him. I played the harmonium.
Mon. 24	It has been a real lovely day. We have led 30 carts & 15 sledges of the park field. We have nearly finished but not quite. The day did not last long enough for us but I think they will finish without me. I am so glad for I have been out everyday for a fortnight. Father & I have milked every night but twice John helped us.
Tues. 25	Another lovely day. Our people have finished the hay, 3 carts, 4 sledges. I have not been out to it at all. J. Wharton came in the first train this morning. He took me by surprised. He helped our people to finish. We had a walk up the Springs this evening. Isabel, Libby & I have set him on his way to the station. It has been a pleasant day.
Wed. 26	It has been a poring wet day. We have been washing. We have been luckey to get finished the hay in time. I have had a letter from Fanny Bragg. She is quite well.
Thur. 27	I have been busy today. We have had lots of strangers on business. Sarah, Bell & Libby went to the Beck Side this afternoon to tea. I went of [*after*] I had done the work. I have got a very troublesome cough tonight.
Fri. 28	It has been showery today. We have had Mr Dormer[131] & son & daughter, each riding on horseback. They got of and came in to the house. Bell & I held their horses. They looked round the barn.[132] We have been down at Sharps tonight.
Sat. 29	A very showery day. Mother, Isabell & Libby have been to Lillymere and the Oax. S,I,L [*Sarah, Isabel, Libby*] & myself have been at Sharps to supper. We have been very busy all day.

---

[131] Mr. Clement Upton-Cottrell-Dormer, the new squire. See 'The Uptons and Dormers of Ingmire Hall'.
[132] the ruined part of the old manor house.

July

Sun. 30   I went with the girls to the Chapel this afternoon and to the Hall Beck tonight. Mr Fayers was their. We have had a pleasant evening. My soul is refreshed. Robert has come back tonight.

Mon. 31   It has been an awful wet day. Father & Sarah have been to Kendal Isabell, Libby & Robert have all gone to their respective homes Mother and [I]have been very busy and the house is feeling like home again.

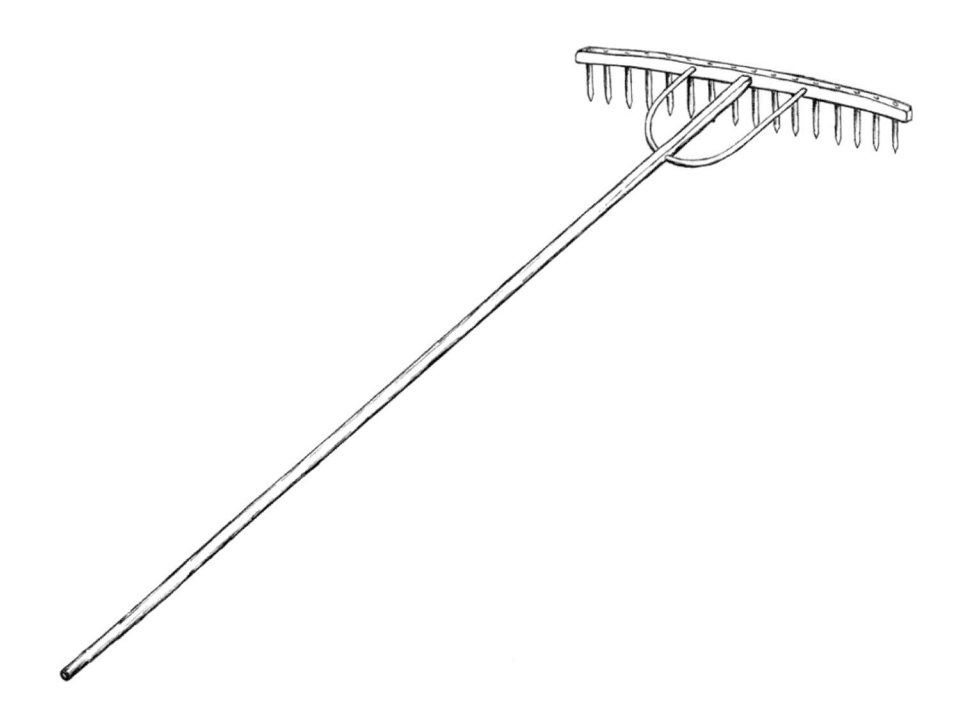

James Wharton & Son

19 January *I have never trusted any one with my great secret yet, but I feel I must write it down here. Well, I am engaged to J. Wharton. I have only known him half a year but it has been love all the time I feel now that I could love him always.*

Agnes Ann's sweetheart, Jim Wharton was a coal merchant working with his father, in what was to become the firm of James Wharton & Son. Often when he called at Killington Hall he was 'on his way from Kirkby Lonsdale' or some other place in connection with the business.

James Wharton senior had set up in business as a coal merchant in the 1840's after leaving his birthplace - Wood End near Tebay (then in Orton Parish), where his father (another James) was a yeoman farmer. In 1851, at the age of 32, James was a 'coal merchant' living as a lodger at Dyke Farm and from there he married Elizabeth Jackson in 1854. James and Elizabeth set up home at Wood End, where their first son James (Jim) was born the next year, before moving into Tebay village. In 1876, the family, including Jim and his three surviving brothers, was living in the village, at Mount Pleasant. James senior was variously described (in the baptismal registers and in local trade directories) as a coal merchant, a grocer, and a dealer in sundries.

When Jim grew up, he joined his father's business ventures. In 1879, James Wharton & Son were coal merchants, grocers, dealers in sundries, and brick & tile makers, the brick works being at Gaythorne, Tebay. Although supplying coal must have been an expanding business at the time, it was clearly not sufficient on its own. Many country people still burnt peat and some who used coal were prepared to collect it themselves from the railway station. An entry in the diary of William Pooley Blacow reads: *'Led 70 cwt of coals from the station. Mr J. Waller and me & T.Richardson join of a truck-load.'*

However, demand for coal delivery would be much greater in the towns and by 1885, the firm had premises in Kendal as well as Tebay. The firm expanded in Kendal and left the Tebay premises to be run as a separate business by one of Jim's brothers, William John Wharton. Meanwhile, Jim and his second wife, Martha, moved to Kendal, where their five daughters and four sons were born.

James Wharton & Son

James Wharton & Son – Depot in Beezon Road, Kendal about 1900.
Photograph courtesy of Mrs. A. H. Lawson

James Wharton & Son

In the early years of the twentieth century, James Wharton & Son of Kendal were coal & coke merchants, lime burners (at Plumgarths, near Kendal), and hay & straw dealers, with an office at 18 Market Place, premises at the Station Yard and a depot on Beezon Road. The Photograph, taken at the Beezon Road depot dates from the early years of the twentieth century.

By 1914 they had added 'hauliers and furniture removers by steam motors' to their list of activities. The original James Wharton of the business title had died and Jim was joined by, and then suceeded by, his son, also James Wharton, who ran the business until his retirement in 1966. In its later years, the firm concentrated on the removal and storage business and the coal trade. In 1966, the removal business was sold and the office in Kendal Market Place became the office of the National Coal Board.

Advertisement, 1930

August

Tues. 1 Showery, very. Uncle James has gone today. Father has been delivering a cow at Sedbergh.

Wed. 2 Another showery day. I have not had much time for reading, although I have had a book in my pocket.

Thur. 3 It has been a very stormy day and it was something dreadful the storm last night. I have had a letter from J.W. [*Jim Wharton*]. He has sent me a bill publishing a trip to Manchester and wants me to go - it is on Saturday - but I cannot.[133] I have returned an answer. I have written to S. [*Sarah*] Clark.

Fri. 4 Rather fine day. Our people have been dipping sheep. My temper has been tried and it has failed.

Sat. 5 It has been a beautiful day. We have been to Kendal - Mother, John & I. Richard has gone home. He went with us. Willie had gone too. Mother & I were in the Exhibition at Kendal.[134] Mother went to see them at the Hall Garth.[135] Sarah Clark was at K. [*Kendal*] with her Father & Mother.[136]

Sun. 6 We have been having a meeting here tonight. Mr. Fayers has been preaching. I have enjoyed it very much. I played the harmonium. T. [*Thomas*] Atkinson & T. Martindale have both been to tea.

Mon. 7 A very wet day. Rather a disappointme[nt] to pleasure seekers.[137] John has been to Kendal with some lambs, Father to Sedbergh with a cow. We have had Mr. & Mrs. Dormer[138] & party. I went to see for them the Church key but could not get it, so they will come again. We are expecting some company tomorrow if its is fine weather.

Tues. 8 It has been a very fine day. It was a very doubtful morning but our visitors came - Mrs Wilson, Mrs Jackson her daughter-in-law, and Jim. He drove them in the phaton. We have had a jolly day of it. I think they have all enjoyed it. I have very much.

---

[133] The reason she could not go to Manchester on Saturday seems to have been that she was intending to go to Kendal that day with her Mother and brother.
[134] The Kendal Industrial and Fine Art Exhibition.
[135] i.e Mother had been to see her son Robert and family.
[136] Thomas [58] & Elizabeth [55] Clark of Orton.
[137] The first Monday in August was a Bank Holiday.
[138] Mrs Florence Anne Upton-Cottrell-Dormer.

August

Sedbergh Station, 1914

Photograph courtesy of Sedbergh & District History Society

August

Wed. 9   I did feel so queer this morning when what I had expected so long had past and gone. Ho this love! Aunt Agnes & Uncle Charley[139] have come back with Father from Sedbergh[140]. It is the first visit since the wedding. I like Aunt far better - wedding seems to have worked a change with her. It is love or something.

Thur. 10   It has been a very beautiful day. I have been picking Cranberries on the Park[141]. M.A. Sharp[142] & I went up together. We started before 9 a.m. [*Mr James*] Sharp & Elenor joined us their. I lost a little shawl in going but I have found it in coming back but such a hunt we have had after it, I have not place in here to tell. I picked about 3 quarts. Albot Fayers has been here this afternoon.

Fri. 11   It has been a very hot day. John and Sharp have started mowing in Dick barn. I have mowed a cart of brackens for Father at the Park barn. Uncle & Aunt have been to Uncle William's for the afternoon.

Sat. 12   A beautiful day. Father drove Uncle & Aunt up to Sedbergh this morning. John has been on for Sharp again. I have been very busy has usual. I have done some gardening. It is looking nice now.

Sun. 13   A real hot day. I have been to School and Chapel. We have had a meeting at Mr Richardson's. Mr Fayers & I walked down from the Chapel together. We had a little private talk.

Mon. 14   It has been an awful hot day. Sarah is not well. Neither was I this morning. I went to Sedbergh Station to meet Jim at the 4 pm. train. He came [*and we*] went up to S. [*Sedbergh*], had our tea in the Independent Schoolroom, a short walk and back to the meeting in the Chapel. It was very good, the singing to. We had a nice quiet walk home. Mother & John were staying up for us.

Tues. 15   It has been a very close hot day. Robert & family were here by half past nine. We have had a jolly day with the little ones.[143] I think they have enjoyed it. Jim has gone back by the 12 past 6 train, after spending the day with us.

---

[139] Robert Kendal's sister, Agnes [46] married Charles Bragg, widower[48] in Liverpool in 1874.
[140] Mr Kendal would be coming back from Sedbergh market as usual on a Wednesday
[141] the Park is now covered by a conifer plantation but is shown on old maps as marshy ground, where cranberries would grow.
[142] possibly Mary Margaret Sharp [11] daughter of James & Elizabeth Sharp
[143] Robert's three children were Lilly [6], Harry [5] and Eliza [3].

August

Wed. 16   We had some thunder earley this morning. John has been leading Will Whitwell his peats.[144] Mother has been to see Jane.[145] She is very poorley, worst she as ever been. I have been rather ill in my health. Mother says it is with being wet on my feet the other day when [we] were cranberreing. I have no appitite much.

Thur. 17   It has been a very fine day but it is awful windy tonight. I have been to Aunt Betty's to finish cleaning for her. She as given me two shillings. I went by the Ox[146] to see Jane. She was something better this morning. Mrs Slinger has been here whilst I have been away.

Fri. 18   We have had Elizabeth, Mary, Johnie and Willie Swidenbank[147]. It has been a fine day but like for a storm tonight. Sarah & I have bethought ourselves we would like to go to Silverdale so, all being well, Mother says we may go next week.

Sat. 19   I have been to Mrs Slinger to get part of a dress cut out. They were awful busy but got my work done.

Sun. 20   It has been a grand day. I have been to School & Chapel. A young man from Kendal, Mr Richard Atkinson, preached.

Mon. 21   Another fine day. We have been very busy. I have had no time for my reading. I have had a letter from Jim to say that he will go with us to Silverdale on Wednesday. Aunt Mary[148] is going too. I hope it will keep fine. We only took the fancy last week to go to see the old place again.

Tues. 22   It has been another fine day. We have been awful busy all day and behind with every thing. I have got into a awful cross way now tonight over trimming my hat. I have got the feather spoiled and been pulling another in. What a bother! Mother has been to see Jane Whitwell. She is improving.

---

[144] i.e. carting peat for William Whitwell.
[145] Jane Whitwell [67], wife of William Whitwell, blacksmith. She died two years later.
[146] The Oaks, Marthwaite.
[147] Elizabeth [17], Mary [12], John [15], & William [14] were four of the children of John & Ann Swidenbank of Whinney Hall, Firbank.
[148] a maternal Aunt: Mrs Kendal's sister Mary Bateman [72] nee Fawcett, widow of William Bateman of Firbank, who was also an uncle of Mrs Elizabeth Sharp nee Bateman.

August

Wed. 23   We got a letter from Mrs Marsden when we were near the station to say she was full of company but S [*Sarah*] & I went forward. Aunt turned back. J.W. met us at Tebay. We passed on by the new line[149] to Arnside S [*Station*][150] and walked to Silverdale from their, calling on our way at Arnside Tower. Jim & I went up to the top. I got a leaf from same for my scrap book. The place is worth a visit. We got very nice lodgings indeed.

Thur. 24   We started off early in the morning, went first to S.S.[*Silverdale Station*] and forward by train to Furness Abby. It is a grand place, worth gowing any distance to see. I cannot begin to discribe it in here. We bought two views &I got an ivy leaf from the Chapel for my scrap book. In coming back we called and stayed an hour in Ulverston then forward to Grange to Mrs. Hodgin's & back by the last train to Silverdale.[151]

Sat. 26   Here I am again at home feeling somehow rather tired, but quite satisfied, feeling with pleasure that home is sweet home. John met us at Kendal. We had a run on the sands before breakfast. It has come on very wet & stormy this afternoon.

Sun. 27   I have been to School & Chapel. We have had such a lot of new scholars lately. We had Mr Trotter preaching at the Chapel this afternoon.

Mon. 28   Showery today. Father & John have been to Kendal with some sheep to the fair. They have heard that Annie Martindale died this morning. She has gone quickley to her eternal rest. I supose she is at peace with God so now will be enjoying the blessed change. She has only been poorley since Easter tea party.

Tues. 29   Showery again. James & Elenor & family should have come today but have not. This is Jim's twenty first Birthday. I do wonder what he is doing and what his thoughts are. I sent him a albertchain of my hair.

---

[149] The Grange & Kendal Line, opened just two months earlier, was built by Furness Railway Company as a shortcut for the transport of coke from South Durham to the Furness blast furnaces. It ran from Hincaster on the LNR south of Kendal to Arnside on the Carnforth to Barrow line. The passenger service on the line was known as 'Kendal Tommy'. The line no longer exists.

[150] Presumably there was no train running east to Silverdale at that time of day.

[151] All the stations used that day are on the Furness Railway's main line from Carnforth to Barrow.

August

Arnside Tower, about 1910.

Silverdale Station, about 1910.
Photographs courtesy of Mr Mike Moon

August

Wed. 30   Mother has been to Sedbergh to a sale. She has bought a feather bed but not b[r]ought it home. It has been a dreadful thunder storm this evening and poring rain. John went this morning to the great Temperance Demonstration at Armethwait Hall, Cumberland.

Thur. 31   It has been a very stormy day. Sharp has been to Sedbergh for Mother & Mrs Sharp's things from the sale. John came back early this morning. He & T. [*Thomas*] Atkinson had stayed all night at Mr Wilson's, Tebay. The Demonstration has not been so good so last year.

Furness Abbey

The Kendal Exhibition

5 August   *Mother & I were in the Exhibition at Kendal*

The 1876 Kendal Industrial and Fine Art Exhibition was held in the Schools of Science and Art from 27 July to 7 September 1876. The first Kendal Exhibition had been held in 1859 in imitation of the Great Exhibition of 1851. The second, in 1872, was reported in the local paper without enthusiasm but on 15 July 1876, The Westmorland Gazette reported:

> 'Kendal Industrial & Fine Art Exhibition. The Schools of Science and Art have been cleared and are now in the possession of joiners, gas fitters and other craftsmen . . . . . The exhibits . . . offer fair to be a decided improvement on the same classes at the 1872 exhibition . . . The number of entries we understand, is over 800, which is considerably more than in 1872 . . . The opening is fixed for Thursday the 27th inst. at half past 2 O'clock in the afternoon, when the borough and one of the county members, along with the High Sheriff, the Mayor and other gentlemen will take part in the ceremony which will be in the Lecture Room of the building. . . .'

The Classes of exhibits included:

wood turning,	shoemaking,	gilding,
glazier's work	saddlers' work,	wood carving,
marble masons' work,	cloggers' work,	water colour,
carpenters' work,	basket-making,	freehand drawing,
cabinet making,	smithing,	bookbinding,
architectural design,	plumbing,	signwriting,
house painters' work,	mechanics,	Photography,
mechanical drawing,	painting in oil,	stuffing,

In addition there was a Ladies' Section, subdivided into fives sections:

     for the Wives and Daughters of Working Men:
     for girls under 16 in such a position in life as likely to become
         domestic servants,
     for girls under 16,
     for children under 7,
and   for General Competition.

Classes for girls under 16 in such a position in life as likely to become domestic servants included:
         a Servant's apron and
         a Specimen of herring bone as shown in Flannel Petticoat.

The Kendal Exhibition

Classes for children under 7 included:
Pinafore, Knitting, Patchwork, and a Chemise for a little girl.

Classes For the Wives and Daughters of Working Men included:

Stocking knitting by elderly women,
Working man's shirt of unbleached cotton,
A full first set of baby clothes,
The most complete set of household linen,
Chemise of bleached calico,
Hearthrug made from pieces of cloth,
Getting up a Damask table cloth and napkins,
Getting up a fine shirt and collar,
Print Dress for a servant made from 8 square yards

Stocking darning,
Stocking knitting,
Patchwork quilt,
Goffering,[152]
Oat cake,
Loaf of homemade bread,

Classes for General Competition (ladies section) included:

Water colour drawing of fruit,
Ladies flannel dressing jacket,
Chalk drawing,
Drawn linen,
Berlin work,[153]
Lace work,
Silkwork,
Quilting,

Foliage or still life,
Fretwork,
Crochet quilt,
Sofa blanket in Wool,
Knitted Bed quilt,
Braiding,
Silk patchwork

and Crochet, Knitting, Netting and Tatting, all in white cotton,

A public presentation of prizes was made in the Town Hall Kendal on the last day of the Exhibition. John Whitwell Esq. M.P. presented the prizes for the General Section and Miss Wakefield of Sedgewick for the Ladies Section. Mr W.H. Wakefield made a speech, in which he mentioned that the rooms were not large enough for the number of entries.

In November, it was announced that the Exhibition had made a profit of £111.11s.5d., and this was to be divided among Kendal Education Committee, the Working Men's Institute and the Christian & Literary & Mechanics Institutes.

---

[152] i.e. crimping with a hot iron
[153] i.e. fine wool embroidery on canvas, producing tapestry-type designs for cushion covers etc.

September

Fri. 1   It has been a splendid day. I had a letter this morning from Mr. Fayers. He is at Brighton staying with Major Way. I was surprised & proud to find Wick Hill[154] on the envelope. He sent me some Foliage leaves. I shall put them in my scrap book. Sarah has been to see Jane [*Whitwell*] - she is a little better. The moon is beautiful tonight.

Sat. 2   Showery. John has gone to Kendal and is going to stay over the week end. I have finished my dress which I have been making. It is a week since we came back [*from Silverdale*]. How time flies!

Sun. 3   It has been a very fine day. I have been to School & Chapel. I was poorley in the Chapel & had to come out.

Mon. 4   John has come home tonight. I have been very busy. I have cut a new dress out for Mother. It is the first I have cut out. Best of all I have had a letter from Robert in America and his Photo. He has revealed a grand secret to me - that is, he is intending being married in October.

Tues. 5   It is very stormy weather. I am busy dressmaking. Our people put the cows into fogg on Friday. I [*was*] in an awful way today for reading. I have been angry too. What a temper I have!

Wed. 6   Busy as usual. I have read a little more this day. My temper has not been so troublesome. There was a sudden death at Sedbergh on Sunday, Jim Brown.[155]

Thur. 7   It has been a moderately fine day. We have had James & Elenor[156] and their two children from Kendal. It was rather late when they came - we had almost given them up.

Fri. 8   It was a lovely morning. Father has been to a sale, T.Cornthwait's near Low Gill. I had an agreeable surprise just before going to milk - J. W. came all unexpected, and it has been such a dreadful shower since he left.

---

[154] Wick Hill, Brighton, the address at which Miss Upton died and the home of her uncle Major Way.
[155] James Brown [32] of Sedbergh.
[156] wife of Agnes' brother, James. The children were Ernest [8] and Ethel [10].

September

Sat. 9   John has been to Kendal with Mother.[157] He has heard that Uncle Thoburn[158] is over from America. Well, Mother has seen him. He should have come to our house from Sedbergh but it was so stormy. He had no more time to spare. He was going back to Liverpool today. I am so sorry I have not seen him.

Sun. 10   I have been to School & Chapel. We had Arthur Fayers[159] preaching. It does feel queer without Mother.

Mon. 11   A very nice day. Sarah has been poorley all day. I have done all the washing myself. I have been busy but I am not tired. It is pleasant having a lot of work when one is in full health. John has been at the fair at Kendal.

Tues. 12   Sarah has not been fit for work again today so I have called myself very busy. I have had the butter to manage & have had no time for reading. By the bye, we received an invitation yesterday for the three of us to a party at Castle How - it is Mary Ann's[160] Wedding next Tuesday. Isn't it jolly, if all is well?

Wed. 13   Our people have been to Borrow Bridge fair. They have bought some sheep. Postman came up this afternoon to keep us company. I have started to net for a pincushen cover. If it is nice, I am going to make a wedding present of it.

Thur. 14   A lovely day. I have been very busy. Sarah has been up at the Fell Side[161] on business. I have longed for a ramble. It has been so delightfully fine.

Fri. 15   Another fine day. I have again been to busy for reading but I have finished that netting. When I finish anything of like that it seemes as though I should have time for anything but it pass through on's fingers to fast.

Sat. 16   It has been another fine day. John has been to Kendal. Mother has come home. I have been busy finishing the pincushen. Mother has brought me lots of couriosites back with her.

---

[157] John took their Mother to Kendal, to stay with one of her daughters, for a week.
[158] This Uncle has not been identified.
[159] Arthur Fayers [24] eldest son of Mr Thomas Fayers, taking the place of his father who was away in Sussex.
[160] Mary Ann Atkinson [36] of Castlehowe, Howgill.
[161] The home of John Kendal (a cousin of Mr Robert Kendal) and family.

September

Sun. 17   I have been to School & Chapel. We had the new minister from Sedbergh, Mr Holroyd[162] preaching.

Mon. 18   I have been very busy all day and now it is very late and I have only just finished a piece of finery, for tomorrow it is the wedding. I do hope it will be fine. It will be quite a novelty in my life.

Tues. 19   It was all we could have could have wished for this morning (the weather I mean) and we were getting on with our work so fast to get off to the Party in good time but, low and behold! the Postman brought John a letter to say the party was put of untill Wednesday. On account of some mismanagement about the licence, they could not be married today. It was a blow but, however, we have it to look forward to.

Wed. 20   It was a dull morning but got out very fine in the afternoon. Father went and got back from Sedbergh[163] before we started. Then we met W. Gibson[164] at a little after two. He rode with us. Their were such a lot of guests at the Wedding but fewer Ladies than gentlemen - 8 Ladies and 14 gentlemen. The house was very small, we had to crush up. Mr & Mrs Capstic[165] left about 7 p.m. for their house & home at Kendal. The party broke up about 1 a.m. It was very good. I enjoyed myself very much indeed.

Thur. 21   It was beautiful morning. Father John Sarah & I started off early for the show at Kendal.[166] I felt has if I had rather stayed at home. I was very sleepy and jaded like and should not have enjoyed it much had not Miss Clarks been their.

Fri. 22   Very busy indeed. Sarah is going to Kendal tomorrow to stay with Elizabeth.[167]

Sat. 23   John has been to Kendal with Sarah and to our surprise he brought W. Atkinson from Cautley & Robert from Burneside Hall.

---

[162] Mr Holroyd was minister at the Congregational Church in Sedbergh. He twice took the service at the Baptist chapel during Mr Fayers' absence.
[163] from the market.
[164] William Gibson [33] of Broad Raine Mill, which the Kendals would pass on their way to Howgill.
[165] Mary Ann and her new husband Edward Capstick.
[166] Westmorland County Show, the agricultural show held in Kendal every September, still attracts people from a wide area - the Kendals met their friends the Clarks from Orton.
[167] Agnes Ann's sister, Elizabeth Gibson [31].

September

They had tea and started off again for Cautley. John has gone by the last train for Orton so their are only three of us at home.

Sun. 24   I have been at School & Chapel. We had Mr. Holroyd preaching again. It has been showery all day and we have had thunder and very heavy rain this evening.

Mon. 25   John came back at noon. He and Father have been with two cows which they have sold, to Sedbergh. Mother & I have been very busy. We have bothe washed & churned.

Tues. 26   A very wet day. It has been the agricultural show at Sedbergh. Father & John have been there with a cow but have not got a prize. T. Martindale has called coming back. I have had the rhumatic very bad in my shoulder all day. I cannot use it properly - never had it so bad before.[168] I have had a letter from M. [*Mary*] Hunter in which she has sent Sarah a scarf.

Wed. 27   A beautiful day it has been. My arm has only been a little better so that it has been difficult working. I have tasted a piece of bridescake. John had some sent from near Cockermouth. Mother & I have been down at Sharps tonight.

Fri. 29   Father has gone to Broughhill[169] with our new horse, so we are only three of us again tonight. T. Martindale has been here tonight. I have parted with two kittens this evening. I have had a ramble up the springs for some licheon, or what I call licheon.

Sat. 30   A very cold black day and it has come on wet tonight. E.A. [*Eleanor Agnes*] Sharp has been up this evening & T. Martindale. Father has come back from the fair. He has sold the horse and come back in the train (last one). Jim Wharton has come with him to stay the week end.

---

[168] Perhaps because of the washing and churning and the very wet weather.
[169] Brough Hill Fair, now known as Appleby Horse Fair.

A Family Wedding

12 September   We received an invitation yesterday for the three of us to a party at Castle How - it is Mary Ann's Wedding next Tuesday. Isn't it jolly, if all is well?

19 September   It was all we could have could have wished for this morning (the weather I mean) and we were getting on with our work so fast to get off to the Party in good time but, low and behold! the Postman brought John a letter to say the party was put of until Wednesday. On account of some mismanagement about the licence, they could not be married today. It was a blow, but however we have it to look forward to.

20 September   It was a dull morning but got out very fine in the afternoon. Father went and got back from Sedbergh before we started. Then we met Mr. Gibson at a little after two. He rode with us. Their were such a lot of guests at the Wedding but fewer Ladies than gentlemen - 8 Ladies and 14 gentlemen. The house was very small we had to crush up. Mr & Mrs Capstic left about 7 p.m. for their house & home at Kendal the party broke up about 1 a.m. it was very good. I enjoyed myself very much indeed.

'On Wednesday the 20th inst., at the Congregational Chapel Sedbergh, by the Revd. H. Holroyd, Edward, eldest son of the late Mr R. Capstick of Low Park Dillicar, to Mary Ann, second daughter of the late Mr R. Atkinson of Castle Howe, Howgill.'
                              The Westmorland Gazette, 23rd September 1876

Mary Ann Atkinson (36), was Agnes Ann's second cousin, a daughter of Richard Atkinson and Mary Atkinson nee Kendal, of Castlehowe, Howgill. Her husband Edward Capstick became a butcher in Kendal. William Gibson of Broad Raine Mill, who accompanied the three Kendals to the wedding, was the bride's first cousin. Like John, Sarah and Agnes Ann, he was unmarried and living at home. If Mrs Atkinson had invited all Mary Ann's aunts, uncles, first cousins and second cousins (to say nothing of the bridegroom's relations), there would really have been a lot of guests, far too many for the parlour at Castlehowe. Presumably only the immediate family attended the Chapel for the wedding ceremony, while the party in the evening seems to have been mainly for unmarried cousins of the bride's generation.

October

Sun. 1   I have been to Chapel this afternoon with Jim and not at the School at all. It has been a beautiful day. I have enjoyed it, more than ever.

Mon. 2   J. Wharton went away by the first train this morning and we have been so very busy all day, both washed and churned, so I am rather tired. I have got a music book by post today which I sent to Liverpool for on Friday.

Wed. 4   Father has been to a sale near Robert's.[170] John has been to Sedbergh. I am so busy and so much work on hand. I have been writing for my Cousin R.K. [*Robert Kendal*] in America.

Thur. 5   Father has been to Kirkby Lonsdale. John has been off after sheep. I have been busy at home. I have sent two newspapers off for America.

Fri. 6   It has been a funny day, very thundery like. It is coming on wet tonight. Father has been to a sale in Dent. John has gone to Kendal tonight after milking time, with Rosie.[171] He is going to Stavely fair tomorrow. I have been busy again.

Sat. 7   We have been expecting Mr Wilson but he has not come but it has been very stormy. John has come back tonight. Something very remarkable has come to me today - it has made me feel quite funny but delighted - it is a wisdom tooth come, the first I have got, bottom left side.

Sun. 8   I have been to Scholl & Chaple. There were only Mr Fayers & I in the morning. I have been copying some poetry tonight. I went by the Oax in the morning to see Jane.

Mon. 9   A very wild day. We have some thunder and very many showers. I helped our people to dip sheep in the forenoon. We have churned this afternoon. I am tired tonight. I have posted a letter for Robert in America. I have sent him my likeness and a white silk pocket handkerchief for a wedding present.

---

[170] Hallgarths near Kendal, the home of Robert Kendal junior.
[171] one of the Kendals' horses.

October

Tues. 10   It was such a delightful forepart of day. I was down at Hall Beck but this evening it has come on such a storm! It was realy frightful when Father was getting the cows in. John has been to Robert's with some sheep & he was out in it. We laid the milch cows and calves in last night.

Wed. 11   A cold stormy day. Mother went with John [when he went to Sedbergh[172]] to the Oax to see Jane and then to see Aunt Betty and he called for her there. Father has been to a sale at Preston Hall. He rode on Sharp's horse, so I was by myself part of the day. I got a letter from J. [*Jim*]. I was nearly provoked to jealousy by a remark which I dare say was only in fun, but I have I hope got the master of the temptation.

Thur. 12   It has been a delightful day. I have helped Father to pick elder berries [*and*] have finished Mother her new apron. Mother & I have been down at Sharps tonight.

Fri. 13   I have been poorley a great part of the day and could not work but I hope to be much better after a good nights rest. I have had a good read today. We have had T. [*Thomas*] Martindale down tonight and have been singing a bit.

Sat. 14   We expected Mr Wilson again but it was such a stormy morning. John has been at Kendal. It is rather a wild night. We have seen some lightning.

Sun. 15   It was rather a stormy morning but has been delightful afternoon and night. I have been at School & Chapel. Mr Fayers gave the children's sermon.

Mon. 16   A moderately fine day. Mother and I & have been washing. I have written to Mary Hunter.

Tues. 17   We have been very busy today. T Martindale came in just when we were ready for supper. He had some with us (a apple dumpling). I have started a pair of stockings to knit myself. I am [*in*] a very bad temper tonight. I cannot help it - Mother has been awfuly provoking today.

---

[172] to market.

October

Wed. 18   A very nice day. Very busy as usual. John has been salving sheep at the Mill. Father & I have had to milk ourselves. We have had the draper traveler from Kirkby [*Lonsdale*]. He has given me a pattern for patch work.

Thur. 19   A nice day. Father has been busy working at the School[173] [*on*] some alterations. John has been at the Mill again. I have planted my hyacinths and tulips, and taken some plants up out of the garden but after all I have not done half has much as I intended.

Fri. 20   We have been very busy & I am tired now. Good night.

Sat. 21   It has been a splendid day. Father has been to Kendal. Sarah has not come back yet. We expected Mr Wilson but he has not come. I have planted another hyacinth which Sarah has sent me.

Sun. 22   It has been a most lovely day. I have been to School & Chapel. We have had M.A. [*Margaret Ann*] & S.A. [*Sarah Alice*] Waller up this evening.

Mon. 23   We have been very busy washing. John has started salving at Sharps. J.W. [*Jim Wharton*] came this evening and stayed untill he thought he should be late for the train and so is going to stay all night.

Tues. 24   A cold day. J.W. went this morning. We have had Mr Allan jun. with some sheep for wintering. I cannot write any more tonight.

Wed. 25   Somehow I have got very little work done today, not so much as I expected but I have read more and feel strengthened in faith. I feel as if I could like to do some thing for Jesus. I am thinking of sending for a collecting card for a good work.

Thur. 26   John has gone to Ravenstonedale this afternoon - their is a fair at Kirkby Stephen. Our big yellow chicken as laid her first egg.

---

[173] The HMI's 1875 report on Killington School stated 'The schoolroom is low and not very convenient. The drainage and ventilation should be improved at once; and the present offices being very confined and too close to the School, new ones [properly separated and separately accessible] should be built.'

October

Fri. 27   We have been busy. Mother is thinking of going to Kendal tomorrow. John has not come back. We are very lonely. I have been practising out of a new music book Jim left the other night

Sat. 28   Father & Mother have been to Kendal. Sarah has come back[174] with them so all is full of news at present. I have got a collecting card which I sent for in aid of the Homes and the report of last year and some little books to distribute.

Sun. 29   I have been to School & Chapel. I have been very successful with my collecting cards. I played the harmonium in the Chapel. This is Mr Fayers' 18 aniversary of is first landing at Sedbergh.[175]

Mon. 30   It has been a lovely day. I have had a letter from Bessie. Father & John have been to Sedbergh fair and to our surprise Robert Clark[176] came back with them, T. Martindale too, and stayed the evening. We have been having some games at cards and a long talk after about all the Orton news. We have been very busy baking oat bread but had to finish up quick towards the later end.

Tues. 31   Hard frost this morning, first we have had this season. Robert left us this morning to go to Rue Crofts.[177] Then we were very much surprised by Mr Dormer coming to ask if the gentlemen could have their lunchone in the hall. There has been a shooting party, so they had is [it] at half past one. It put us in a bit of a flutter. John has gone to Sedbergh tonight to the Bible society's meeting.

---

[174] Sarah had been away for five weeks.
[175] Mr Thomas Fayers [53], Baptist minister, came to Sedbergh in 1858 to serve the navvies building the railway.
[176] Robert Clark [32], brother of Sarah and Libby Clark.
[177] a farm in Marthwaite.

Ingmire Hall, 1922
Photograph courtesy of Sedbergh & District History Society

The Uptons and Dormers of Ingmire Hall

30th January   We have heard today that Miss Upton is dead and was found dead on Thursday morning the 27th. I suppose her heart had been given to the Lord some time since so she will be living in glory now, for she has had her share of affliction.

'Deaths: On Thursday 27th ult. at her residence, Wick Hill, Brighton, Miss Upton of Ingmire Hall Yorkshire, aged 43 years.'
The Westmorland Gazette, 5th February 1876

Above the front door of Killington Hall are the arms of John Upton and the date 1803, although the Hall is much older than that. The Upton family owned Ingmire Hall in Marthwaite and a large estate of farms on both the Yorkshire and Westmorland sides of the River Lune. In her Will, Miss Eliza Frances Upton was described as 'of 22 Palace Gardens, Kensington, Ingmire Hall, Sedbergh, and Wick Hill near Brighton'. The Executor and main beneficiary was her uncle, Mr Gregory Lewis Way of Wick Hill, but the Ingmire Hall estate was in trust in the Upton family and passed to Florence Anne Upton, who had married Clement Cottrell-Dormer, from Oxfordshire. The couple took the surname Upton-Cottrell-Dormer and, after Miss Upton's death, they moved into Ingmire Hall.

28 July   We have had Mr Dormer & Son & Daughter each riding on horse back. They got of and came in to the house. They looked round the barn.

7 August   We had had Mr & Mrs Dormer & party. I went to see for them the Church key but could not get it, so they will come again.

31 October   We were very much surprised by Mr Dormer coming to ask if the gentlemen could have their lunchone in the hall. There has been a shooting party so they had it at half past one. It put us in a bit of a flutter.

10 December   We had Mr Dormer and a Mr Way at the [Sunday] School. We were rather confused but they were very good. Mr Way taught a class of boys.

It appears that Mr Dormer and Mr Way took an interest in the Baptist Chapel and Sunday School founded by Miss Upton and her protege, Thomas Fayers. But he had retired by 1881 and use as a Baptist chapel eventually ceased. In 1902, Mrs Florence Upton-Cottrell-Dormer arranged for major alterations to the buildings, converting the Sunday School into living accommodation and transforming the character of the chapel by the installation of contemporary stained glass windows. The chapel was transferred to the Church of England and is now known as St. Gregory's, Vale of Lune.

November

Wed. 1   This has been a jolly day. It is morning now - half past twelve. Mrs Fayers[178] & Maddie[179] came this afternoon and are staying all night. Mrs F. is so full of chatter, we have been hearing some long tales. We have a fire in the Hall and have had some games and quirkery. I was busy baking the forepart of the day.

Thur. 2   I have taken my dalias up. Mrs Fayers and Maddie started off home soon after breakfast. I have got a dreadful bad cold. I am awful sleepy tonight.

Fri. 3   We have had quite a change in the weather. It is very wet tonight. The children at the School have been barring the master instead of the 5st. There has been some fearful rows.[180] My cold is not much better.

Sat. 4   This is the bonefire night. Mother and I have been up on the Horse Hills to see. We have seen two or three, and to my great surprise who should come in first after us but Jim! He is staying over the weekend.

Sun. 5   My cold is so bad I have not been to School or Chapel, or rather that has been an excuse, James[181] & I have been for a short walk. Mrs Sharp has been up this evening. Altogether I have enjoyed the day.

Mon. 6   It has been a lovely day. We have been very busy washing. I have received a letter from Cousin Robert in America. He as written it before he has got my last. J.W. left us this morning for the first train. I have been in a good way for working. I am determined to get a lot of sewing out of my hands this week.

Tues. 7   A cold frosty day. We have had a great strainger today, Uncle Henry Rishton.[182] I never saw him in our house before. He has

---

[178] Eliza Fayers, [52], born at Pimlico, wife of Thomas Fayers, the Baptist minister.
[179] Madelaine Fayers, [15] daughter of Thomas & Eliza Fayers.
[180] a custom normally carried out at the School on 5th November, moved to the 3rd in 1876, because the 5th fell on a Sunday. Agnes Ann seems to use the word 'rows' to indicate noisy, boisterous behaviour rather than arguments.
[181] This is the only time in the diary when Jim Wharton is called 'James'. Usually 'James' means Agnes Ann's brother, while her sweetheart is 'Jim', or 'J.W.'
[182] Henry Rishton had an engineering works in Kendal, making kitchen ranges. He was married to Agnes' Aunt Elizabeth, sister of Robert Kendal.

November

some work to do at the Parson's house. We had two of his workmen too, to see for lodgings. We are going to have them next week.

Wed. 8 It is very cold. We have some snow tonight, the first of the season. Father went[183] to Kendal fair today. He has not come back, is going to stay all night. The two workmen which we expected next week have come today, unexpected. I have been writing to Sarah Clark, tonight.

Thur. 9 John went to Kendal this morning with the conveyance. Father and he have bothe come back tonight. They have bought a stag.[184] We have had the Postman to tea this afternoon. I have had a Dear Letter today.

Fri. 10 A beautiful day, very frosty. We have been down this evening to see through the Parson's house. It is not finished yet.

Sat. 11 It is a awful cold night, such a strong cold wind. I am almost perished with cold. John is finishing salving at Sharps.

Sun. 12 It was such a dreadful stormy morning it was doubtful wether it was wise for me to go or not but in the end I went (to *Sunday School*). There was only Kate & I, none of the men in the morning & only one in the afternoon. As I was going I had such a tumble in the Cross Bank and hurt my knee.

Mon. 13 It has been such a dreadful cold and windy day.

Tues. 14 A very stormy day, rain and wind together. All the trees are looking very bare and leaves are lying about in heaps. We have had Wm.. Sharp & John to supper and Thomas came in after. We have had some fun - they are having their martinmasing.[185]

Wed. 15 Quite a chainge in the weather this morning. Their had been a lot of rain during the night. I have finished three sewing jobs off

---

[183] John went to Kendal next morning 'with the conveyance', so Mr Robert Kendal must have gone on horseback.
[184] a young, unshod pony.
[185] i.e. the farm workers had come home for a brief holiday around the quarter day of Martinmas (11th November).

November

today. John, Sarah & I have been down at James Waller's[186] tonight. We have been introduced to Mr Whittingdale, the School Master.[187]

Thur. 16   It has been a nice warm day. We have been very [*busy*] cleaning upstairs as I am going off[188] on Saturday. I have had a letter from Mary Hunter and a Photo of her's. It is very good. They have got into their new house.

Fri. 17   We have had Postman to tea. Mrs Edmonson came up this afternoon with a pair of new boots. I'll see how long they will serve me. John, Sarah & I have been down at Sharps tonight. I am going off tomorrow. I have heard that old Mr Wilson died a week last Thursday.

Sat. 18   Here I am tonight at the Edge Bank,[189] but it has been as usual with me - I have had such adventures, first of all I never saw any of them from here at Kendal and found it out that Joe[190] had gone and left me but I have not space to tell how I did get here but they had never got my letter.

Sun. 19   Libby, Josie[191] & I were at the Church in the morning but I cannot gather the sweetnes from the Church as I can from Medthody. Mary, Sarah[192] & I were at a meeting at Garthrow. One of the Mr Rhodes was the speaker.

Mon. 20   It has been a lovely day. I have kept in the house all day too. They have been busy washing and after[*wards*] dressing corn - quite new work to me. I have done a lot of talking. Joe has been at Martons tonight so we have been by ourselves.

Tues. 21   It has been a lovely day, clear and frosty. Elizabeth & I have been to Selside Hall this afternoon to see Isabela Ann.[193] She has gone to live a servant their. It is her first service place. It is a

---

[186] James Waller [65], farmer of Beckside, formerly of Hallbeck, Killington.
[187] See 'The Village School'.
[188] it was Agnes Ann's turn to go to Kendal to stay, but for only two weeks.
[189] Edgebank Farm, Skelsmergh, home of Agnes Ann's eldest sister, Mary Airey.
[190] Joseph Airey, husband of Mary.
[191] daughters of Joe and Mary Airey, nieces of Agnes Ann.
[192] Sarah [11] another daughter of Joe and Mary Airey.
[193] Isabella Ann Airey [18] eldest daughter of Joe and Mary Airey, niece of Agnes Ann.

November

very old fashoned house. They did not make any fuss over us. We went to see the Church and I got a leaf to put in my scrap book. We had a long walk and saw a lot of the country which was new to me.

Wed. 22   A nice day. E. [*Elizabeth*][194] & I have been to Lavric Bridge[195] to see Mrs Dixon. We met with a very hearty reception indeed. It is a beautiful house and so nice and clean. The worst of it, we had such a short time to stay. She gave me two shillings for my collecting card, more by half than I expected. Mrs Dixon gave me a very pressing invitation to stay with her a few days when I come this way again, also we had each our pockets filled with apples. I am very much pleased with our visit.

Thur. 23   It has been a fair day. I started off from Edge Bank about a 1/4 to 3 and arrived at Hall Garths at 4 p.m. I have had a very nice walk. I enjoyed it very much all along through Burneside. Mary gave me 1 shilling to my card - I am getting on very well.

Fri. 24   I lift Hall Garths about 2 p.m. and came to Aunt E. [*Elizabeth*] Rishton's and spent the afternoon and evening. I have enjoyed it very much. Uncle[196] was so cheerful. He took me through their works and especialy to see their furnaces and I saw the melted iron put into moulds and more than I have space to tell, and the lads were very good - they showed me all kinds of fancy work.

Sat. 25   This indeed has been a day of stirings. I stood with some eggs in the Market for Mary and helped her to do some shopping. I have not been down to the Gibsons[197] at all. It has been wet tonight. Lucy[198] & I have been with T.Atkinson[199] from Howgill & W.A.[200] from Cautley & J.W.A.[201] at a marionet but I dont want to go again - its nothing. Wet tonight.

---

[194] Elizabeth / Libby Airey [16], daughter of Joe & Mary Airey
[195] Laverock Bridge, Skelsmergh, near Kendal.
[196] Henry Rishton of 47 Stricklandgate, kitchen range maker & hot water engineer. Uncle Henry and Aunt Elizabeth had ten sons but only the younger ones were still at home.
[197] 163 Highgate, the home and butcher's shop of James & Elizabeth Gibson and family
[198] Lucy Atkinson [15] of Kendal, second cousin.
[199] Thomas Atkinson [34] of Castlehowe, second cousin.
[200] William Atkinson [22] of Cross Hall, Cautley, a nephew of Richard Atkinson, of Castlehowe.
[201] John William Atkinson [21] of Finkle Street, Kendal, second cousin.

November

Sun. 26   I was up early this morning but had no one to go to Chapel with, so did not get to any. I went down to Gibsons[197] after dinner to see them. Then Lucy & I & a Miss Capstic went to W.A.'s [*William Atkinson's*] Cliff Terrace[202] to tea. J.W.A.[*John William Atkinson*] & W.A. [*William Atkinson from Cautley*] were there too. We had a nice sing and then some of us went to Chapel. We have had a good sing since.[203]

Mon. 27   Rather a dull sort of day. I was out with Elizabeth[204] shopping this afternoon. I called to see the Parkers[205] and got an invitation for tea tomorrow afternoon. Lucy & I have been about since. Margaret[206] was down and we took her back. We have been awful silly since. It's very late now to be only coming to bed.

Tues. 28   I was down at Elizabeth's in the morning and [*had*] dinner with them. Bessie [*Parker*] called for me up here to go for a walk. We went on the cannal banks to Haws Bridge and back by Natland. We had a look round the Churchyard. I got a leaf from it, also one from Haws Bridge. We had a splendid walk indeed. I had tea with Bessie and enjoyed myself very much.

Wed. 29   This indeed has been a wonderful day! In the morning I went to Aunt E's [*Elizabeth's*][207] and on my way back I was in a shop with my back turned to the door and who should get hold of my shoulder but Jim! I was taken by surprise and best of it he had not seen me before he got into the shop. He went back with a train about 12 a.m. I walked with [*him*] to the station and was back again for dinner. Wether any of them suspected me or not I do not know but it required some effort to keep green. I have been to Mrs Capstic's[208] to tea this afternoon.

---

[202] William Atkinson [56] of 10 Cliff Terrace - a retired bootmaker, a widower, born at Sedbergh but not a member of the two Atkinson families who were Agnes Ann's cousins.
[203] By this time, Agnes Ann seems to have been staying in Finkle Street with her second cousins, the Atkinsons, neighbours of her brother James.
[204] Elizabeth Gibson [30], of Highgate, Kendal, Agnes Ann's sister.
[205] The household of Bessie Parker, with whom she stayed in February.
[206] Margaret Atkinson [29] of Kendal, second cousin.
[207] Elizabeth Rishton [54], Robert Kendal's sister, married to Henry Rishton.
[208] probably Mary Ann Capstick whose wedding party Agnes Ann attended in October.

November

Thur. 30   It has been a beautiful day. I was out about the town in the forenoon. This afternoon, J.W. [*John William*] Atkinson, Lucy, Mr James & I have been to Stavely at a tea party connected with a new Chapel (Weslyan). We all enjoyed it and, to say for myself, I never enjoyed a teaparty better considering who was missing. We saw the Church [*and*] I got a leaf from the Churchyard. Dr. Millburn, a blind man, was the speaker.

Kitchen Range in Rishton's works, Stricklandgate, Kendal, from a Photograph in the Margaret Duff collection.

The Parsonage

2 April — I was at this Church in the morning ... Mr Thompson was preaching. He landed back yesterday to Mansergh.

16 May — We had Jimie Atkinson called to see us this evening. He has been helping to move Mr Thompson's furniture.

5 July — I supose this is to be Mr Thompson's wedding day today.

7 Nov.ember — We have had a great strainger today, Uncle Henry Rishton. I never saw him in our house before. He has some work to do at the Parsons house. We had two of his workmen too, to see for lodgings. We are going to have them next week

8 Nov.ember — The two workmen which we expected next week have come today. They came unexpected.

10 Nov.ember — We have been down this evening to see through the Parsons house. It is not finished yet

'On Mon. 3rd inst at SS Philip and James, Oxford, the Rev. Horace Vincent Thompson, Incumbent of Killington near Kirkby Lonsdale, to Annie, widow of George Hosmer Esq. late of Rohilcund, NWP India.'

The Westmorland Gazette, 8 July 1876

Killington Parsonage was enlarged and improved in 1876 at a cost of £599, raised by donations from funds such as Queen Anne's Bounty and the Diocesan Church Extension Society, plus gifts from private individuals, including £50 from Miss E.F.Upton.

Agnes Anne's Uncle Henry Rishton was a kitchen range manufacturer & hot water engineer with premises in Stricklandgate, Kendal, so that the work carried out in November by his workmen probably consisted of kitchen fitting and plumbing as finishing touches to the extension. It appears that Mr Thompson's furniture had been moved out earlier in the year and perhaps he had been lodging in the neighbouring parish of Mansergh since the spring. He must have brought home his bride in July to his temporary accommodation.

Dr. Milburn's Lecture

30 November   *This afternoon, J.W.Atkinson, Lucy, Mr James & I have been to Stavely at a tea party connected with a new Chapel (Weslyan). We all enjoyed it and to say for myself I never enjoyed a teaparty better considering who was missing . . . Dr Millburn a blind man was the speaker.*

1 December   *I . . . went to Mrs. Parkers in the afternoon to tea. I left them early on account of going to a lecture at the Wesleyan Chapel given by Dr Millburn, the Mayor in the chair.*

Advertisement in the Westmorland Gazette of 25 November 18

WESLEYAN CHAPEL, STRICKLANDGATE, KENDAL.
"What a Blind Man Saw in England"

A LECTURE on the above subject will be delivered by the Rev. W. H. MILBURN, D.D., the celebrated Blind Orator, late Chaplain to the Congress of the United States, on Friday, December 1st, 1876.

Chair to be taken by the Mayor, H. WILSON, Esq., at 7 30.p.m.

A Collection at the close on behalf of the Ambleside Home Missions.

And a report on 9 December 1876:

'On Friday week a blind American clergyman, the Revd Dr. Milburn, gave a singularly interesting lecture in the Wesleyan Chapel, Kendal, on 'What a Blind Man Saw in England'. The Mayor presided. A collection was taken towards defraying the expense of furnishing a ministers house at Ambleside, and amounted to £13.12s.2d.'

December

Fri. 1   It has been a very dull wet day. I was in the house all morning and went to Mrs Parker's in the afternoon to tea. I left them early on account of going to a lecture at the Wesleyan Chapel given by Dr Millburn, the Mayor in the chair. Miss Brunskill from Windermere has come to stay all night. We have had such rows.[209] John William has given three of us each a half penny for going to bed.[210]

Sat. 2   Here I am again att Home. Father came for me today and I am glad to be back home again. It is so nice and quiet after the bustle of the town, but I have enjoyed myself very much indeed [and] have seen and learned many new things.

Sun. 3   I have been to School & Chapel. We had a very good Sermon from Mr Fayers. Mr Dormer was there. Thomas Sharp has been up tonight. We have had a good sing.

Mon. 4   We have been busy washing. John has been to Kendal with some sheep.

Tues. 5   We have been very busy again. I have been ironing with candle light. We have been making our mince meat. It has been a strange day. Sarah has been in a bad mood all day. We had a packman & Sarah bid at a white counterpane and got it. Then she would lay it onto me but Mother took it and gave it to John. I have been awfully put out with it. I hope it will be gone by morning.

Wed. 6   Father has not been at Sedbergh today. John took the butter on to the Mill. I have been busy baking but it is a thing I like very much. I have been awful sleepy and awfully bad tempred tonight and in no working way at all.

Thur. 7   It has been a lovely day. I have been busy in the sewing way. I have finished knitting a pair of stockings tonight. James from Kendal and Ernest[211] came with their conveyance in the afternoon. Father has gone back with them - their is a great fat show[212] tomorrow at Kendal, so I am going to sleep with Mother.

---

[209] the word 'rows' is again used for commotion rather than quarrels.
[210] John William Atkinson [22] - the three to whom he gave a halfpenny would be his brother Richard [18], his sister Lucy [16] and Agnes Ann.
[211] Agnes Ann's brother James and nephew Ernest [8].
[212] that is, a show of 'fatstock', beasts ready for slaughter.

December

Fri. 8 — It has been another beautiful day, rather frosty. I have got a lot of sewing work done. I have been in a good working way. Father has come home.

Sat. 9 — A dull day. I have written and posted a letter for Cousin Robert Kendall in America. I have been busy making some alterations with my waterproof jacket.

Sun. 10 — I have been to School & Chapel. We had Mr Dormer and a Mr Way[213] at the School. We were rather confused but they were very good. Mr Way taught a class of boys. We had Mr Trotter to preach.

Mon. 11 — We have had Uncle C [*Charles*] Bragg[214] with a letter from Aunt Ann[215] in America to say Uncle Thomas[216] is dead. I will write tomorrow more about him. John has been killing Robert a pig.

Tues. 12 — Sarah & I have been down at Sharps tonight. Uncle Thomas died on the 22nd of October, only being a week and three days ill, inflamation on left lung, and bilious fever, aged 59. He was buried the day following.

Wed. 13 — It has been a lovely day. It is quite frosty.

Thur. 14 — Another beautiful day. I have sent my collection to E.W.Thomas, the secretary at London I have got £1.8s. in all. I have been round Killington this afternoon begging for our Sunday School. I have got 10s.6d and my tea at Mrs Gotts.[217] Jim has come this evening. He is going to stay all night.

Fri. 15 — A fine dry windy day but no frost. J.W. [*Jim Wharton*] had to hurry off in the morning. I have been quite busy all day. Sarah & I have been down at Sharps tonight. I have a letter from Sarah Clark inviting the three of us for Christmas. It will soon be here.

Sat. 16 — Sarah and John have been to Kendal. It is very cold and windy tonight.

---
[213] See 'The Uptons and Dormers of Ingmire Hall' and 'The Vale of Lune Chapel'.
[214] Charles Bragg [49]. Aunt Ann must have written the letter to Aunt Agnes, whose husband, Charles Bragg, brought it to Thomas's brothers in Killington.
[215] Aunt Ann may have been Uncle Thomas' widow or his sister Ann Kendal [50], who has not been traced in England and could have emigrated with Thomas.
[216] Thomas Kendal, Robert Kendal's brother.
[217] Stangerthwaite, Killington

December

Sun. 17   I played the harmonium in the Chapel this afternoon. We had a capital sermon, [*from*] Mr Fayers. I was surprised to see Mrs Clark there. She pressed us very much much to go at Xhmas.

Mon. 18   A very cold day, dry but not freezing but I hope it will before Xhmas. I have been awful busy all day. After we had done washing, I cleaned the seller and Buttery. I have written back to Sarah Clark acknowledging[218] her kind invitation. I have got my scarf finished and have got my hair back in a twist which I sent to Liverpool.

Tues. 19   Rather a fine day. We had Miss Dormer and an other Lady this afternoon with cards of invitation one for Father to a tennents' dinner at Ingmire Hall on the 2st January and another for Mother, Sarah & I for tea and Xhmas tree on the 4th Jan. It was a surprise. It is something quite new and delightful.

Wed. 20   I got the receipt [*for the money*] I sent to the Homes, London, yesterday and today I have got a little book sent from there. I have been awful busy. I have finished my sheet[?] and tonight I have been working hard to finish a piece of embroidery. It is very late now.

Thur. 21   A wet stormy day. It is Mrs Sharp's birthday. I sent her a mince pie for a present. Father has been to Kirkby Lonsdale fair. I have been very busy again. All being well, I am going to Orton tomorrow.

Fri. 22   I started from home, Father taking me to the Station in a thick snow shower, arrived at Tebay allright. Mr Wilson & Jim met me there. I stayed with Mrs Wilson untill the concert which was very good but which I did not exactly apreciate. Robert & Sarah were there. We had a very cold wet drive home.[219]

Sat. 23   I have been helping Libby[220] to make black puddings. They had killed their pig yesterday. I have had a jolly day & has learned lots of things. Our John has come in this evening to stay over

---

[218] By 'acknowledging', Agnes Ann probably meant accepting. Although the invitation was for the three of them, Sarah Kendal did not go to Orton for Christmas. Agnes Ann and John travelled separately, Agnes Ann on 22nd. and John on 23rd.

[219] i.e. to the Clark's house at Orton.

[220] Libby /Elizabeth Clark [26].

December

Xhmas. Jim & other gentlemen have been spending the evening with us.

Sun. 24   I was with Mr. & Mrs. Clark[221] & Robert[222] at Chapel. T. Moffat preached at [as] the stated minister was absent. I was not at the Church in the afternoon but we have been to Chapel tonight.

Mon. 25   It has been very Christmas like - all is covered with snow and freezing. Sarah, Mrs Clark, & John, with me, were at Church in the morning and John, Libby, Sarah & I walked to Gaisgill in the afternoon. We had our tea there. Robert went at night to the lecture. It was not a very excellent one. We had a nice walk home.

Tues. 26   John went with Robert, L. & S. to the station. He has gone home, they to Miss H. [Hester] Scaifs[223] Wedding in Middleton.[224] Mrs Clark and I have been to the Primitive teaparty. It was a very good lecture. Miss Morphet has come back with us.

Wed. 27   Miss Morphet & I had a long talk in bed last night or rather this morning about religion. They have come back from the wedding very sleepy and tired. I have started knitting a jacket like Mrs Clark's.

Agness Ann Kendall
Killington Hall
1876

---

[221] Mr Thomas Clark [58], farmer of The Park, Orton, & his wife, Elizabeth [55]
[222] Robert Clark [32] son of Thomas & Elizabeth Clark
[223] 'On Tues. 26th inst. at the Parish Church Kirkby Lonsdale by the Revd.H.W. Scaife, brother of the bride, assisted by the Revd. Canon Ware, M.A., vicar, Thomas Ephraim Nicholson of Melton House, Highgate, London, to Esther, youngest daughter of the late R. Scaife of The Park, Orton.'
The Westmorland Gazette, 30 December 1876

Orton Town Head, in the snow. Late nineteenth century. Photograph courtesy of Mr John Falshaw

Christmas

Gaisgill Chapel Christmas meeting

25 December   *It has been very Christmas like. All is covered with snow and freezing. Sarah, Mrs Clark & John with me were at Church in the morning and John, Libby, Sarah & I walked to Gaisgill in the afternoon. We had our tea there. Robert went at night to the lecture. It was not a very excellent one. We had a nice walk home.*

'On Christmas Day the annual Sunday School festival took place in the Wesleyan Chapel at Gaisgill near Orton and after the appetites of the juveniles had been satiated with tea and its accompaniments, visitors partook of the refreshing beverage. The public meeting held in the evening was numerously attended and suitable addresses were delivered.'

The Westmorland Gazette, 30 December 1876

Christmas

The party at Ingmire Hall

19 December   We had Miss Dormer and an other Lady this afternoon with cards of invitation on for Father to a tennents' dinner at Ingmire Hall on the 2st January and another for Mother, Sarah & I for tea and Xhmas tree on the 4th Jan. It was a surprise. It is something quite new and delightful.

Both events were reported in the Westmorland Gazette:

The tenants' dinner, with 60 guests, took place in the specially decorated servants' hall and was followed by speeches, toasts and entertainment by Sedbergh Brass Band and a party of glee singers from Sedbergh.

> 'On the 4th inst., the wives and children of the tenants, numbering in all about 100, were invited to tea. A grand Christmas tree was set in one of the rooms, and a plentiful supply of oranges and other fruits was given to the children.'
>
> The Westmorland Gazette, 13 January 1877

Memoranda

6 December   *I have been busy baking but it is a thing I like very much.*

18 December   *I . . . have got my hair back in a twist which I sent to Liverpool.*

At the end of the Diary, Agnes Ann wrote some memoranda:

<u>Plain Loaf</u>

three cupfulls of flour,
butter size of an egg,
one cupfull of sugar,
one cupfull of milk,
candid lemon to taste,
one spoonful and a half of baking powder,
an egg if chosen.

Amerous Lilly

Mrs Williams
4 Upper Duke Street
Liverpool

Mrs Jane W. Williams [40] of 4 Upper Duke Street, Liverpool was the wife of Robert Williams, hair cutter, employing five assistants. Their daughter was described as a wig shop assistant. No doubt this was the address to which Agnes Ann sent a length of her hair, to be made into a twist.

Epilogue

17 January 1876   *Time flies. This is Bessie Parker's 21st birthday. I wonder w[h]ere I shall be on mine. What a dark future!*

On her 21st birthday, 10th February 1879, Agnes Ann Kendal was still living with her parents at Killington Hall, and she remained there for a further three years, while both Sarah and John married and left home.

The day before her 25th birthday, Agnes Ann Kendal married James Wharton at the Congregational Chapel in Kirkby Lonsdale. It was six and a half years since she first met him at Orton Pot Fair. The couple lived at Tebay where Jim was still working in his father's business as a coal agent.

But '*What a dark future!*' The next winter, Agnes Ann Wharton, expecting her first child, developed scarlet fever. On 5th December, she gave birth to a son, James Kendal Wharton, but three days later she was dead. The baby lived only a fortnight. They were buried at Orton.

Note in the Wharton family bible:

'James Wharton married Agnes Ann Kendal of Killington Hall at Kirkby Lonsdale on Feb'y 9th 1882. Died of scarlet fever, her and the baby, died in Dec. 1882'

Jim Wharton married again. He and his second wife, Martha, moved to Kendal and had nine children. In old age he still spoke fondly of the outings he had enjoyed with Agnes Ann during their long courtship. But no Photographs of his first wife were kept in the Wharton family. There is no gravestone for Agnes Ann and her son in Orton churchyard. This book is her memorial.

Epilogue

James Wharton
1855 - 1942

Photograph courtesy of Mrs Helen Lawson

Sources

Main Sources

The 1876 diary of Agnes Ann Kendal.
The Westmorland Gazette, 1875, 1876, 1877 and 1882.
Census records for Killington, Kendal and Sedbergh.
Parish Registers of Killington, Sedbergh and Orton.
Annual Reports on Killington School at the Kendal Record Office.

Other references:

'The Farming Diary of William Pooley Blacow' transcribed by Mr J. A. Goulding. Extracts were published in The Sedbergh Historian, 1989, 1990, 1993, &1997. Use has also been made of unpublished research lodged by Mr Goulding with SDHS.

'The Ancient Parish of Kirkby Lonsdale, Its Churches and Endowments' by the Bishop of Barrow in Furness. Published by Charles Thurnam & Sons,1890.

'Mine Eyes unto the Hills - Places of Worship in Sedbergh and Surrounding Dales' Edited by Mary Gladstone; Sedbergh Christian Festival, 1995.

'The Pot Fair and the Tup Fair at Orton' by Horace Wilson in 'Memories of Orton, a Westmorland Parish Remembered' 1998.

'Cumbria's Lost Railways' by Peter W. Robinson. Stenlake Publishing.

'Historic Farmhouses in and around Westmorland' by J.H. Palmer. The Westmorland Gazette 1945.

Index of people mentioned in the Dairy

AIREY, Miss Elizabeth / Libby   14,17 Feb.
 17, 23, 25, 27, 29, 31 July, 19, 21 Nov.
Miss Isabella Ann / Bell   17, 22-3, 25 July,
 27-9, 31 July, 21 Nov.
Joseph / Joe   20 Nov.
Miss Josephine/ Josie   19 Nov.
Mrs Mary   12 Feb.,19, 23, 25 Nov.
Miss Mary Agnes   17 Feb.
ALLAN, Mr., junior   24 Oct.
ATKINSON, Miss Elizabeth /Bessie   24 Feb.
George   5 March
James /Jimie   16 May
Miss Jane /Janie   24 Feb.,16-19 April
John William   15-6 Ap., 21 May, 25-6, 30 Nov.
Miss Lucy   7 June, 25 -26, 30 Nov.
Miss Margaret   7 June
Miss Mary Ann   12, 20 Sept.
Richard [cousin]   15-16 Apr., 2 May,
 10 Jul., 5 Aug .
Mr Richard   20 Aug.
Thomas of Castlehowe,   6 Feb. 6 Apr., 6, 31 Aug.
 25 Nov.
Thomas, formerly of The Hill,   6 Mar., 18 May
William, of Cliff Terrace,   26 Nov.
William of Cautley,   23 Sept., 26 Nov.
BATEMAN, Mrs Mary   21, 23 Aug.
Miss Mary Ann   9, 11, 13,17, 26-7, 31 Mar.,
 5, 7, 10 April
BLACOW, Miss Grace   25 Jan., 23 Feb.
BLENKHARN, Annie   19 April
BENSON, Mr.   20, 24, 26 Apr,
 13 18, 30-1 May, 14, 23 June
BRAGG, Mrs Agnes   9, 11-2 Aug., 11 Dec.
Charles   9, 11-2 Aug., 11 Dec.
Miss Fanny   17, 18 May, 7, 26 July
BROWN, James / Jim   6 Sept.
BRUNSKILL, Miss   1 Dec.
BURTON, Mr   19 March, 23 July
CAPSTICK, Edward   20 Sept.
Mrs Mary Ann   20 Sept. 29 Nov.
Miss   26 Nov.
CLARK, Mrs. Elizabeth   5 Aug, 17, 24-7 Dec,
Miss Elizabeth / Libby   9 Apr, 1 July, 21 Sept.
 23, 25-7 Dec.
Robert   30-31 Oct.22, 24-27 Dec.
Miss Sarah   5-7 Jan., 7,10 Feb., 10 Mar.,
 9 Apr, 5,28 June, 1,17 July, 1,5 Aug.,
 21 Sept., 8 Nov., 15,18,22,25-27 Dec.
Thomas   5 Jan., 5 Aug., 24 Dec.
COCKSHUT, Miss M   23 April
CORNTHWAIT[E], T.   8 Sept.
DAYTON, G[e]orge   25 Feb.
DIXON, Mrs   22 Nov.
DORMER, Mr Clement Upton-Cottrell-   28 July,
 7 Aug., 31 Oct., 3,10 Dec.
Mrs Florence Anne Upton-Cottrell-   7 Aug.

EDMONSON, Mrs   17 Nov.
EL[L]IS, George   20, 28 Jan.
Mrs Mary Ann /Polly   28 Jan.
Richard / Dick   28 Jan.
FARRER, Thomas   19 May
FAWCETT, Robert Kendall   28 Mar,10 Apr,
 26 May, 8 July, 5 Oct., 6 Nov.
FAYERS, Albert / Albot   10 Aug.
Arthur   10 Sept.
Mrs Eliza   2 March, 1-2 Nov.
Miss Madelaine L.   1-2 Nov.
Thomas   2,9,23,30 Jan., 6,13,20 Feb.,
 2,5,12 Mar.,16,23 Apr., 7,14 May,
 9,14,30 July, 6,13 Aug., 1,10 Sept.
 8,15,22,29 Oct., 3,17 Dec.
GELDERT, Mrs Mary Agnes   17 Feb.
GIBSON, Miss Edith   4, 8,18 July,
Mrs Elizabeth   22 Sept., 21-2, 27-8 Nov.
Miss Elizabeth   4 March
James   25-6 Nov.
Miss Margaret / Maggie   4, 8-9,16,18 July.
 27 Nov.
William,   16,31 Jan., 2 Apr., 26 May,
 7, 22 June, 20 Sep.
Miss   28 Feb.
GOTT, Mrs   14 Dec.
HARRISON, Nicholas   17 Jan.
HAYGARTH, Robert   9 April
HAYTON, Jim   19 Jan., 15 April
HINDSON, Mr   5 April
HODGINS, Mrs   24 Aug.
HOLROYD, Mr   17, 24 Sept.
HOPE, Revd. R.D.   27 Feb.
HUNTER, Miss Mary   22 Mar., 25-8 Apr.,
 1-3,15, 25 May, 2 July, 26 Sept.,16 Oct.,16 Nov.
JACKSON, Mrs   8 Aug.
JAMES, Mr   30 Nov.
Thomas / Tommy   3 July
Thomas / Uncle   17 July, 1 Aug.
KENDAL, Mrs Ann   11 Dec.,
Mrs Elenor /Eleanor   29 Aug., 7 Sept.
Mrs Elizabeth / Mother   passim
Ernest   7 Sept., 7 Dec.
James   5, 11 Jan., 24 Mar., 6 Apr.,
 14 July, 29 Aug., 7 Sept., 7 Dec.
Mrs Jane / J.   28 June
John [brother]   passim
Robert , junior 1 Mar., 1 June, 4,10 Oct.,11 Dec.
Robert / little Robert   17, 23, 30-1 July
Robert senior / Father   passim
Miss Sarah [sister]   passim
Thomas   11, 12 Dec.
William   14 April, 11 Aug.
LEWTHWAIT[E], Janie   20 May
Miss Mary   14, 17, 26 May
MARSDEN, Mrs   23 Aug.

109

Index of people mentioned in the Dairy

MARTINDALE, Annie   28 Aug.
Thomas   13, 22-3 Jan., 26 Feb., 7, 20, 26 Mar.,
   21, 30 Apr.,13, 25, 29-30 June, 6 Aug.
   26, 29-30 Sept., 13,17, 30 Oct.
MEDCALF, John   3 July
MILBURN, The Rev. W.H., 30 Nov., 1 Dec.
MOFFAT, T   24 Dec.
MORPHET, Charles / Charley 10 June
Miss Mary Ann / Polly   28 Jan.
Thomas   3 Feb., 2 May
Miss   26-7 Dec.
NELSON, John   12,14-5 April
PARK, Hannah   11 Feb.
PARKER, Mrs Bessie   17 Jan., 5,7,10 Feb.,
   15 May, 30 Oct, 27-28 Nov., 1 Dec.
PARKINSON, Miss Agnes   10 April, 10 May
John   10 April, 3,7 June
POTTER, William   31 Jan.
RADCLIFF[E], John / Jack   31 Jan., 2 Feb.
RICHARDSON, Mr   21 Jan., 15 Mar.,13 Aug.
RISHTON, Mrs Elizabeth / Aunt E.   24, 29 Nov.
Henry   7, 24 Nov.
RIGG, T   15 May
RHODES, Mr   19 Nov.
SCAIF[E], Miss Hester/Esther   26 Dec.
SCHOFIELD, John   15 Jan., 3 Feb.,
SEDGWICK   3, 7 April, 28 May 11,14 June
SHARP, Miss Eleanor Agnes / Elenor   22 Feb.
   1, 30 Mar., 22,24 May, 23 Jun. 10 Aug. 30 Sep.
Mrs. Elizabeth   7, 26 Jan., 2, 22 Feb.,
   7,9,11,13, 17-8 Mar., 5 Nov., 21 Dec.
James   14,20,22 Jan. 4,7,13,18 Mar.,
   25 Apr., 31 May, 10-2, 31 Aug., 11 Oct.
John   8 June, 14 Nov.
Miss Mary / M A   10 Aug.
Thomas   14, 28 Jan., 11 Feb.,14 Nov., 3 Dec.
William   28 Jan., 11 Feb., 8 June, 14 Nov.
SHARPS   11,14,31 Jan., 2,22,28 Feb.,
   3,10,15,22,25,27,29 Mar., 7, 28 Apr.
   27 May, 9 June, 3,28-9 July, 27 Sept.,
   12, 23 Oct., 11,17 Nov., 12,15 Dec.
SHEPHERD, Mrs Elizabeth / Betty   16 Jan.,
   15, 22 June, 17 Aug., 11 Oct.
S. or L.   16 Jan.
Mr   19 June
SLATER, Henry   2 Mar., 26 April
SLINGER, Mrs   5, 7 April, 17, 19 Aug.
SOMERVELL / SOMERVILLE, Frederick   17 Feb.
Mrs Mary Agnes   17 Feb.
SWIDENBANKS, Mrs Ann   31 March
Elizabeth, Mary, John & William 18 Aug.
THOBURN [Uncle]   9 Sept.
THOMAS, E.W.   14 Dec.
THOMPSON, the Rev. Horace Vincent   2, 20 Ap.,
   16 May, 5 July

THORNBORROW, Thomas / Postman   22 Jan.,
9,10 Feb.. 11 Mar., 5 Apr., 13,19 Sep., 9,17 Nov.
TROTTER, Mr   27 Aug.,10 Dec.
UPTON, Miss Eliza Frances   30 Jan., 13 Feb.
WALLER, James 25 Jan., 20 Apr.,1 May,15 Nov.
Miss Margaret Ann   13 Jan. 23 April, 22 Oct.
Robert   28 Feb.
Mrs [Margaret]   28 Feb.
Miss Sarah Alice   13 Jan. 23 Apr, 10 May, 22 Oct.
WAY, Gregory Lewis   10 Dec.
   Major   1 Sept.
WHARTON, James / Jim   passim
Philip   8 Feb.
WHITTINGDALE, Mr, 15 Nov.
WHITWELL, Mrs Jane   12 Apr., 21, 29 July,
   16, 17, 22 Aug., 1 Sept., 8, 11 Oct.
William, senior /Will   16 Aug.
William, junior / Willie 10 July, 5 Aug.
WILKINSON, Mrs Isabella / Bella   28 April
Miss Mary Jane   1 May
Robert   1 May
Thomas / Tommy   8 April
WILLAN, George   25 Jan.
Mrs Grace   25 Jan.
WILLIAMS, Mrs   18 Dec. & See "Memoranda"
WILLIAMSON , Mr E.C.C.   14,17 Feb.
WILSON, Mr   14-15 Jan. 4,18 Mar., 29 Apr.,
   7,13 May, 10 July, 31 Aug.,
   7,14,21 Oct., 17 Nov., 22 Dec.
Mrs   19 June, 8 Aug., 22 Dec.
WINSTER, James   17 Jan.